Beauty through Health

FROM THE EDGAR CAYCE READINGS

Beauty through Health

FROM THE EDGAR CAYCE READINGS

COMPILED BY

Lawrence M. Steinhart

ARBOR HOUSE
New York

THIS BOOK IS HUMBLY DEDICATED
TO THE BEAUTY WITHIN EACH
AND EVERY ONE OF US—
WAITING TO BE PERCEIVED.

CONTENTS

CONTENTS

*Beauty comes from within, rather than
as an external condition—for the external
fades, but the beauty of life, of individuality
shining through that personality of self,
gives the beauty that fades not. . . .*

*As to the physical appearance, and the
outward show of face and figure, necessary
that these be modeled after that of the self's
ideal, that these may manifest that the
body would radiate through its inner being.*

Edgar Cayce

THIS IS a refreshing, new approach to beauty that threads together the philosophy of the Edgar Cayce readings. The author, Lawrence M. Steinhart, famed international beauty authority, has been a connoisseur of beauty for many years, dedicating his life to enhancing the female image.

His approach is direct. First, dealing with the physical recommendations for beauty, he gives suggestions for a lovelier skin, hair, nails, teeth, feet, make-up, removal of blemishes, etc. He revels in the dietary suggestions and Edgar Cayce's 'old fashioned remedies' for healing various ailments (a trend which seems to be growing more popular these days), discusses oil massages and packs and adds a word of caution about proper eliminations.

Lawrence's next step through the Edgar Cayce mirror of beauty takes you to a reflection of the inner self and the concept that "Mind is the Builder" (that attitudes and emotions can make you healthy and beautiful, or ugly and sick) and poses the theory of reincarnation by explaining that *you* are the expression of what you have built in this body from many past lifetimes.

He has envisioned a 'total concept' of beauty and health, based on the physical, mental/emotional and spiritual philosophy from the "wisdom of the readings." As Director of the Chiropractic Research Division of the Edgar Cayce Foundation during the past five years, and being involved in considerable research on health and disease, I find a definite parallel between the concepts of beauty and health, which reverberate—TOTALITY.

In the Aquarian Age, healing will encompass *all* healing arts, working to achieve balance for the total person. There is no one healing profession today that includes all of Edgar Cayce's concepts. The various professions involved in good health must necessarily cooperate with one another to achieve this end. A constant nutritional program suited to the individual should be of primary concern. This will sometimes require the cooperation of an M.D., for some herbs and tonics require medical prescriptions. However, many of the herbal tonics given by Cayce could be made at home. A balance must be brought to the cerebrospinal and autonomic nervous system through the suggested techniques of chiropractic, osteopathy, naturopathy, naprapathy, lymphatic massage, physiotherapy, spinal oil rubs, external packs and poultices and hydrotherapy. Balance in the endocrine system is affected by healthy attitudes and emotions,* by everyday activities such as work/play, exercise/rest, and finally by the spiritual activities of man through prayer and meditation.

Thus Lawrence's recommendations for 'total beauty' go far beyond the applications for the physical body. He invites you to listen to good music, to surround yourself with a vibratory aura of perfume, color and light, to choose your favorite gems and stones, to record your dreams, listen to your astrological influences, and to radiate beauty and joy in simply "serving others."

The author fascinates you with the prospect of your own potential beauty, then leads you through a maze of controversial issues with such skill and finesse that as you arrive safely at the end of his rainbow, your pot of gold is an 'aura of beauty' radiating the energy and love of the Christ light within.

GENEVIEVE M. HALLER, D.C.
Virginia Beach

* *Jeffrey Furst, Edgar Cayce's Story of Attitudes and Emotions,* (New York: Coward, McCann & Geoghegan, Inc., 1972).

Preface and Acknowledgments

WHEN EDGAR CAYCE, fully awake, regarded beauty, it was with the eye of a professional photographer. He might have used as his yardstick the 'fashionable face of the moment'. In sleep however, his eye for beauty measured in universal perspective. The entranced seer saw beauty then as a threefold law: beauty of body, beauty of mind and beauty of spirit, all linked inseparably together.

It is the purpose of this book to present an approach to beauty given through the prophet of the Aquarian Age, an expanded concept of total beauty, perceived by all the senses, some of which we are not yet fully aware.

In an age where the jealous guarding of secrets, political, trade or otherwise—has become a way of life, how can one explain an Edgar Cayce? What motivated him to offer his knowledge and secret formulae? The answer can be found in the readings themselves.

"You have recipes all your own. Keep them. But give them away if you would keep them. For remember, you can never lose anything that really belongs to you, and you can't keep that which belongs to someone else. No matter if it is spiritual, mental or material, the law is the same." (3654-1)* "Know that what is *truly* thine *cannot* be taken away from thee; nor is any real character ever lost." (2448-2)

All women—regardless of age or position—will respond to something that promises to enhance their looks. Is it wrong or frivolous? Surely this depends upon the purpose. "It is up to the entity, then, in its experience, in its associations with

___

* The names of the persons having readings have been replaced by numbers to retain anonymity and to insure privacy. The first number represents the person; the second represents the number of the reading given for that person.

others, in its dealing with opportunity with others, with conditions and circumstances, to use all in a constructive way and manner and, when there are those periods when disturbance and disappointments come, to have in the spiritual ideals, the mental and mental purposes, that which will keep the body from seeking only gratifying of physical appetites." (5250-1)

The source of Cayce's knowledge was the Universal Storehouse of all knowledge. He was able to answer questions relating to the creation of man, universal law, all physical laws in the earth and could solve the most complex health problems in which man had become enmeshed. Yet he answered with the same care what appeared to be the most trivial questions about aids to beautify a body. He would show equal concern for a minimal flaw, such as a wart, as he would for something far more serious. Though our problems vary, each is of uppermost concern to the one who has to deal with it personally.

Certain rules for living wove their way through the readings, leaving no room for doubt as to the best choice of action. Biblical truths were given: "Do what is at hand, line upon line, precept upon precept." Cayce knew that if a simple facial flaw was bothering a body, its removal would change the mental outlook which, in its chain reaction, would have positive effects on the more serious problems of the body. "For the beauty of man's mind is oft directed by the beauty of his environs." (1771-2)

Most interesting and meaningful, perhaps, were the health patterns which emerged from groups of readings, indicating that specific habits have their polar retribution. Between the constant encouragements for beneficial activities and the reprimands for neglected ones, there were many specific do's and don'ts for those fortunate enough to have had personal readings. But we can all benefit from those rare times when Cayce gave the advice that "This would be good for ANY body." A great favorite is: "Those who would take a peanut oil rub each week need never fear arthritis." (1158-31)

In researching the readings, now clearly indexed, it is a simple matter to locate all references on a given subject, after which one can draw his own conclusions. This author, through his life experiences as a professional beauty consultant, has been well acquainted with the problems of people seeking to be beautiful. Thus the readings have been scanned for answers to the most often asked questions on problems which are most prevalent in the field of beauty.

It is not the purpose of this book to tell anyone what to do, but to offer you, the reader, the benefit of my experience in the world of 'beauty consciousness' which has been immeasurably expanded by seven years of research in the Cayce readings.

A few years ago, I shared the confidence of one of the great beauties of the world, an English baroness who had spent thousands of dollars for cellular treatments at a Swiss therapy clinic. Afterward she was informed that there were a number of things which she would have to do *herself* in order to insure the success of the treatment. To her annoyance, there was a list of must-do's which included adherence to a diet of restricted alcoholic intake (small amounts of red wine were permitted), little if any red meat, fresh air and exercise, ten hours of rest a day and NO SMOKING. All of these suggestions have been repeated time and again throughout the Cayce readings and one does not have to be a wealthy baroness or go to a Swiss clinic to benefit from them. The rules of balanced living are there; all we need to do is to apply them.

Read on. The gems are yours for the taking. Make them your own and let your beauty radiate to brighten all around you.

Grateful acknowledgment is made to Hugh Lynn Cayce for sowing the seed of this book in the mind of the author, and for the invitation to write it.

To Thelma Barret, a living example of Beauty à la Cayce, whose inspiration and help gave this book its initial impetus.

To Tom Johnson, whose help in making available so many of the items mentioned in the readings facilitated the researching of this book.

To the ARE staff members, whose help also made the research that much easier.

To the visitors to the ARE headquarters in Virginia Beach, whose smiling faces made the future audience of the material come to life in the author's mind.

And last, but not least, Beth Blasko, without whose constant encouragement and faith this book would never have been completed.

It is not the purpose or the intention of this book to diagnose or prescribe for any specific ailment; this is merely a report of the author's findings from his research of the Edgar Cayce readings on subjects related to beauty and health. It must be borne in mind at all times that the remedies and health aids enumerated in this book were recommended for specific individuals, and although the suggestions and formulas comprise only items which may be obtained without a prescription, responsibility for any and all attempts to research said suggestions and formulas as reported must lie with the reader.

Beauty through Health

FROM THE EDGAR CAYCE READINGS

About Edgar Cayce

To FULLY appreciate this book, one must know something of Edgar Cayce, the psychic who has captured the attention and interest of America and the world. While still in school, Edgar Cayce exhibited foreshadowings of his extraordinary talent. By the age of thirteen, having read the Bible once for each year of his life, he had a vision of a lady—complete with wings—who told him that his prayers had been heard and asked him what he wanted most of all, to which he answered: "To help sick people—especially children."

As a child, Edgar Cayce was a particularly poor student, and one evening, while his father was trying to drum a spelling lesson into his tired head, the lady reappeared to him in his thoughts. He imagined that he heard her saying that if he would sleep, she would be able to help him. He slept on his speller and upon awakening found that he knew not only the day's lesson but the whole contents of the book. From then on, armed wtih his new learning technique, his grades improved considerably.

An encounter with a famous hypnotist as a young man started the chain of events which uncovered his psychic gifts. Edgar, suffering from severe hoarseness, was "put under" by the hypnotist in an attempt to cure the condition by suggestion. Although he was able to speak while under hypnosis, upon awakening he was still hoarse. Repeated attempts by the hypnotist and subsequently by a doctor failed to cure him. The third person to hypnotise him, however, met with favorable results. Cayce was asked, while in the sleep-state of hypnosis, to diagnose his complaint and suggest a cure, to which he responded perfectly and thereafter was able to enter the sleep-state by himself.

The next experiment was to see if he could diagnose the ailments of other people and suggest cures. This triggered the discovery of Edgar Cayce's powers, the true scope of which was not to be appreciated for many years.

Although Edgar Cayce's formal education was confined to grammar school, when in the self-induced sleep-state, he was able to answer any question posed—on any subject. He had the ability to thoroughly examine *any* body and diagnose its problems. Furthermore, the person did not have to be present to benefit from his extraordinary psychic gifts, he or she simply had to request an appointment. The psychic discourses—the responses to these requests—were called 'readings'.

Cayce never knew what he was saying when in the sleep-state, and fearing—in the beginning—that his medical advice might prove harmful to the one receiving the reading, he insisted that his words be taken down and a doctor consulted before acting upon the suggestions. He soon learned to trust the readings, especially after they cured his wife, Gertrude, who was suffering from tuberculosis, and saved the eyesight of his son after an accident which the doctors assured him would leave the child sightless. It is because of his initial insecurity about the dependability of his source that his legacy to the world is nearly fifteen thousand documented readings.

Readings to correct physical ailments constituted the first nineteen years of Cayce's work until he met one Arthur Lammers, a wealthy printer from Dayton, Ohio, who enlarged the scope of the readings by posing questions which others had hitherto failed to associate with his powers, such as metaphysics, esoteric astrology, philosophy and psychic phenomena. It was during these readings that a subject arose which gave Edgar Cayce's formal Christian upbringing its most severe jolt: reincarnation.

A breakdown of the readings shows that 8,976 were physical, 2,500 were life readings (the tracing of a person's past lives),

799 business, 667 dream interpretation, 401 mental-and-spiritual, 24 home-and-marriage and 879 miscellaneous readings. However, each reading contained material which covered a multitude of subjects.

The abundant supply of information which came through the Edgar Cayce readings sparked the formation of the Association for Research and Enlightenment (ARE) which is an open-membership, nonprofit organization chartered under the laws of Virginia to carry on psychic research. Its work is to disseminate the knowledge which Edgar Cayce gave. This is accomplished through its many membership activities, lectures, seminars, conferences and study groups. It is one of the largest organizations in the world devoted to the research and study of psychic phenomena and, through the subject matter in the readings, finds itself linked with all people who seek the truth, including those in the fields of medicine, psychology and theology.

From the readings emerged answers to riddles which have puzzled mankind for countless years. There emerged a new understanding of the human body and its intricate workings. Cayce seldom put a name on the trouble, saying that names merely gave the trouble metes and bounds. As he stressed the individuality of each entity, he treated the patient as a whole person and not as a collection of categorized ailments. Sometimes he would ignore the *symptoms* completely, knowing that when the *cause* was eliminated, the symptoms would disappear of their own accord. Most important of all, perhaps, was the emergence of a complete philosophy regarding the question of man's existence, a question which has remained incompletely answered by even the world's greatest thinkers.

It is from this source that our information on the subject of beauty has been gathered, a source which more than adequately provided the answers.

Part I

THE OUTER

MAKE UP IF YOU MUST

CAYCE NEVER actually recommended make-up per se. Perhaps he understood the fickle nature of fashion. The dimensions of beauty with which he dealt could not be applied with a paintbrush. One learns from the readings that beauty begins with an inner harmony at the core of the individual and radiates to the four corners of his universe. Expressing that harmony, Cayce suggested keeping a joyful attitude and being: "Ever a worker, as the bee—yes, BUT IN THAT WAY IN WHICH IT IS EVER A CONTRIBUTION TO MAKING THY PORTION OF THE EARTH A MORE BEAUTIFUL PLACE FOR MEN TO LIVE IN." (3374-1)

It has been proven, in make-up and grooming programs in psychiatric clinics, that the use of cosmetics has a deeper value than may appear on the surface. If a woman who has been deeply depressed for a long period is shown by the proper application of make-up that she can become attractive, her new acceptance of herself becomes an experience that is both emotionally and psychologically uplifting. Apropos of this, the French poet, Jean Cocteau, in a communication to a fellow cosmetologist expressed it thus, "If there is a defect on the soul, it cannot be corrected on a face. But if there is a defect on the face, and one corrects it, it can correct a soul."

Any woman is raw material for the make-up palette, though make-up is not plastic surgery. It is illusory and should be the transparency through which one's individual personality shines and emerges, rather than a mask which hides an inferiority complex and creates a character which is not the real you.

Step one: before you start painting, have a clean canvas. Look at your face as nature gave it to you, without make up, in a large mirror. Accept what you see. Your face is yours. It is unique, it is individual.

Cayce speaks of entities. What is an entity?

"The entity is that combination of the physical body throughout all its experiences in or through the earth, in or through the universe, and the reactions that have been builded by those various experiences or the spiritual body of an individual. That which is individual. That which is the SUM TOTAL OF ALL EXPERIENCE." (262-10)

Avoid the pitfall of identifying yourself with a mental image of someone else. Beware of the facsimile. For there is a tendency on the part of many women to identify their facial type, their features, with someone whom they admire, often overlooking their own admirable qualities. This deplorable attitude aspires to the achievement of a façade which merely simulates a personality which is not their own and does not permit the individuality to shine through.

Asked about twin souls, Cayce answered:

"That there are identical souls, no. NO TWO LEAVES OF A TREE, NO TWO BLADES OF GRASS ARE THE SAME. They are the complement one to another, yes." (3285-2)

"Look on the individuality of the individual . . ." (2582-3) For ". . . each soul is a universe in itself." (1096-4)

Women have been persuaded by the cosmetic industry to categorize their face shape, skin type and features, limiting by the very definition God's custom styling. The first thing to do is throw out the misconception that faces are shaped by geometric design. There is not such thing as a triangular, rectangular, square, round or marquise-shaped face. Your face contains all possible shapes. It has curves and angles, flat surfaces and curvilinear ones. It reflects and absorbs light and shadow at unpredictable points, which change as you smile, change with every movement of the eyebrows, every expression. Somehow, that face of yours will not fit into a select mathematical pattern to suit the classifications of a geometrician.

Just how much can be done with cosmetics? The next thing to throw out is the idea of the 'perfect' feature. Your features are perfect for you when you allow them to exist in harmony. Realize the potential of your own face, its power of emotional expression, its inner beauty, its frankness, its reflection of inner spiritual strength which you have earned yourself through your own experiences, and you will never again have to be reminded of the hollowness that is achieved by becoming a facsimile of others. The mutability of the human face was finely stated by Sir Francis Bacon: "There is no beauty that hath not some strangeness in the proportion." And this is the starting point for your first objective look into the mirror.

The point of your first long, clear look into the mirror: to realize and FULLY appreciate the plastic qualities of your face, and to bring it within the area of your sensitivity and taste. Your face is more than just bone structure and features created by skin, cartilage and fibrous tissue. It is mobile; nature builds, destroys, mutates, builds anew. Not a single cell in your body can be considered a permanent part of you.

". . . the body replenishes itself every seven years, and there is a continued growth in not only the structural portion but of each center, each fibre, each atomic influence . . ." (735–1)

This transitory, plastic quality of what you may have heretofore considered to be immutable is what governs our approach to make-up now. In other words, a recognition of the constantly changing character of your face, of the natural processes which will enable you to combat the destructive forces that can drag you down and negate all that vitality, beauty and expressive power that is within you.

This new, enlightened way of looking at yourself, in the re-evaluation and realization of your own qualities, is the mental broom with which you will sweep clean the effects of time, fashion, the elements, your work and possibly your slavish imitation of others.

The best antidote to a false approach is nature's make-up: a pleasant smile. Try it in front of your mirror. A relaxed, easy smile, thinking of green pastures, of hammocks, of lazy afternoons, of anything that helps relieve the tension. Now the easy smile. Watch the corners of your mouth go up. Watch your eyes light up—and make sure they do. After that, the cosmetic treatments which follow are merely for the enhancement of that which you have already begun to project from within yourself. The best make-up in the world cannot compensate for the beauty which is yours alone, waiting for you to acknowledge it.

CHAPTER *2* *What the World Sees*

THE CLEANSING AND CARE OF THE SKIN

GRASPING AT a cosmetic as a cure-all for facial ills, when the most it can do is provide a cover-up or camouflage, is facing life as an ostrich faces danger. Burying the head in the sand will not make the danger disappear—nor will covering a flaw on the skin make *it* disappear.

"Don't depend on cosmetics to clear or purify the skin" (5271-1) Cayce told one young woman when she asked what cosmetics would be best.

Realizing what cosmetics can do and cannot do should be the first step toward using them. Ideally, a clean, healthy skin is the prime requisite if cosmetic application is to be successful from an esthetic viewpoint. However, the health of the skin is a chain reaction stemming not only from the health and cleanliness of the body, but also from the mind.

Cleanliness is more than just an external wash, it is a multi-level affair, for are we not multi-level beings? It could be described as a spiral of habit patterns which affect our being. For instance, our mind and attitude as we sit down to eat affects our choice of food, as well as the action the food will have on our bodies. The elimination of this food—or lack of elimination and its consequences—results from the mind's action upon the body as well as the physical actions which govern our daily habits.

Whenever Cayce was asked what to do first, he would say "Begin where you are, do what is at hand." So let us begin with the part which the world sees first: the outer skin.

Soap

To soap or not to soap has long been a controversial question among dermatologists and cosmetologists alike. Some would never permit soap to touch the face, others would use nothing else, while some merely voice reservations about it.

It is interesting to note that the first record of the use of soap in history was in ancient Rome, where it was used *not* as a cleansing agent for the skin but as a hair dye! Most of us have been using soap all of our lives, despite the admonitions of some beauty empresses who warned that its use would irreparably damage the skin.

At this point let us consider the rationale of dirt. What is dirt? Where the skin is concerned it begins with the secretion of waste matter—and dead cells—which the body does not require. The body eliminates this through the pores of the skin and sebaceous glands. By nature it is an oily or fatty substance and the cleansing of it is best achieved by dissolving it.

If you have ever picked up tar on the soles of your feet at the beach, you know that you can scrub and scrub with little effect. But just a quick massage with a cream, oil or some other solvent will literally melt it away. Certain types of soap dissolve the dirt on some skins better than others, while dryer skins require a cream now and then—if not always. If cleansing is not carried out properly and consistently, the waste matter hardens and remains in the skin. It becomes more and more difficult to remove, thus creating what magazine ads delicately refer to as 'impurities in the skin.'

Cayce recommended both soaps and creams. Individual people respond to different treatments. The soaps which were recommended were Woodbury, Camay and Palmolive among others.

To 1532–3 he cited Ivory as being for her "the better or purest." Castile soap was the one most often recommended. A Castile soap is one which has a base of olive oil and is so named because Castile, Spain, was where it was first made. There are many fine brands of Castile soap available both in liquid and solid form. When 2072–6 asked what soap would be least harmful and most helpful in correcting and beautifying the skin, she was told:"Pure Castile soap is the better as a cleanser."

For one middle-aged woman with tendencies toward muscle atrophy Cayce suggested creaming the face and neck to help keep firm muscles, then added that this would be done "After a thorough cleansing with any good toilet soap, preferably that prepared with Olive Oil or Coconut Oil rather than other character of fats." (3051–3)

For use with the soap, 2072–16 asked if it would "be advisable for the body to use a brush for washing face and neck?" She was told: "A sponge, but not a brush." For those of you who have never washed your face with a sponge, do *not* underestimate its strength. Let your first sponging be a gentle one until you feel how much your skin can take. Some skins are more delicate than others.

In one reading in particular, soap was given as the ideal deodorizing agent:

Q. "What deodorant and anti-perspirant would be effective and unharmful for this body?"

A. "The use of the pure soaps is preferable to any attempts to deodorize. ANY that allays perspiration certainly clogs the activity of the respiratory and perspiratory system. And the activity of the glands closest, of course, under the arms and between the thighs or limbs, is that which causes such conditions. Then the more often there is the use of the bath or the soap and water, the better it is."

Q. "What ingredients in such preparations are harmful?"

A. "Anything that closes the pores of the skin to prevent perspiration." (2072-6)

A healthy skin requires not only a thorough outer cleansing but depends to a large extent upon the factors of proper nutrition, exercise in the fresh air and a healthy emotional attitude.

Apropos of our concern for the mental attitude, Cayce cautioned 1928: "There is nothing outside of self half so fearful as that that may be builded or brewed within self's own mental and material being." And to 348: "Be constructive mentally, don't build poisons as fast as you eliminate them."

Creams

Seeking advice for correcting and beautifying the skin, a woman was told, "As a cleansing cream or the like, the Black and White products are nearer to normal." (2072-6)

What was meant by "nearer to normal"? Was it the acid/alkaline balance or the nature of the oils used in the cream? "As a cream or base for the better conditions of face, arms and limbs," Cayce told a young woman with a susceptibility to skin problems, "we would use the GENUINE BLACK AND WHITE preparations. These are preferable to most of the compounds that carry leads or poisonous conditions for the skin." (2154-2)

Tests have shown Black and White creams to be alkaline reacting, and a number of readings endorsed this factor when prescribing the cream. In one reading, Cayce summed it up this way: "we find that a cream that is less acid will be more beneficial. A test of these may be easily made before they are used. Both the red and blue litmus tests are the better way for testing same. And any that is wholly alkaline and non-acid is preferable." Later Cayce was asked about another company's products. "Make the test for them," he said, "and these will be found to vary at times, even as those that have been indicated that are among the best, but USE ONLY THOSE THAT ARE ALKALINE REACTING." (275-37) "Those that have been indicated that are among the best" surely confirms what many women have long suspected: that high cost and fancy packaging is no guarantee of quality.

The blue and red litmus paper Cayce refers to is available at most drug stores but it is somewhat less sensitive than the newer Nitrazine paper. With Nitrazine it is possible to obtain an exact Ph reading almost instantly. However, either paper can be used to test not only beauty products but your own system as a means of keeping it in balance. (See Chapter 6)

Oils and fresheners
Skin fresheners, or astringents, as they are sometimes called, are used after cleansing the skin, usually after a cream cleansing. Their function is to remove any excess cream from the pores, refine them and leave the skin feeling refreshed. The ones made with menthol, camphor and a high alcohol content, which cosmetologists recommend for oily skin, have a pore tightening effect. Some fresheners incorporate a tiny amount of oil for the dryer skins, while others contain glycerine.

Witch Hazel, extract of the plant *Hamamelis virginiana,* has been used as a skin lotion, or the base of a skin lotion, for years. Frequently it turns up in the readings as an ingredient of a massage compound. For instance, after prescribing a special cleansing treatment for a young woman with skin eruptions, Cayce further advised, ". . . then following same, massage into the skin a compound as follows: Camphorated Oil, 2 parts; Witch Hazel, 1 part; Russian White Oil, 1 part. This will, when shaken together, make a tendency for clearing the skin, you see?" (528-2)

Very cold water patted on the skin has a tightening, invigorating effect, and is a good substitute for a freshener occasionally. But a woman who was apparently using water too often was assured by Cayce that the substitution of a skin freshener instead of so much water "would be very well." (2582-2)

A seemingly perfect skin freshener that is all things to all people—excellent for both dry or oily skin—is a recipe that was obligingly given: "To one half pint of Olive Oil, add one ounce of Rosewater, a few drops of glycerine and one ounce of a 10 percent solution of alcohol [pure grain], and shake these well together, this is a skin invigorator." (404-1)

An effective skin freshener composed mostly of olive oil is a concept that is hard for the cosmetologist, raised in the oil-for-relaxing, alcohol-for-stimulating school to accept. But the concept works! What could be the logic? That the olive oil is heavier than the oils secreted by the sebaceous glands and thus displaces them? That its nature dissolves sebum which has hardened in the pores? Is the olive oil more natural to the skin than the oils which are thrown off? A woman suffering from over-acidity was told by Cayce to take internally, "Oils a plenty, Olive Oil WELL for the body." (482-2) Alkaline activity is certainly indicated here.

In one important reading Cayce spotlights olive oil and reveals its true worth: "OLIVE OIL—PROPERLY PREPARED (HENCE PURE OLIVE OIL SHOULD ALWAYS BE USED) —IS ONE OF THE MOST EFFECTIVE AGENTS FOR STIMULATING MUSCULAR ACTIVITY, OR MUCOUS MEMBRANE ACTIVITY, THAT MAY BE APPLIED TO A BODY . . ." (440-3)

This presents a whole new picture of why olive oil was recommended so highly—and so frequently—in the readings for both external and internal use. (See Chapters 6 and 8)

Number 288-38 wanted to know the cause of her dry skin. She was told: "The poor circulation." Number 274-9 asked, "What causes a dry and scaly skin? Should this condition be remedied locally as well as generally, if so how?" She was told that "this may be aided by the rubbing with a combination of Rose Water and Olive Oil—equal parts. This is to soothe the skin, but the general applications should be from within."

Closing the pores of the face has become such a routine fetish that Cayce's advice to a young girl to "use such cosmetics as do not become too great astringents" seems at first rather strange. (1206-15) But in a reading for another person some light was shed on the matter. "More capillary circulation needed," Cayce explained, "so that the drosses and the eliminations are not discharged in the superficial activity through the pores where the body is attempting to breathe in, as it were." (850-2)

Another cosmetic rule falls by the wayside when we find Cayce answering the question "Is it well to remove matter from the pimples and blackheads that form?" with a matter-of-fact "This is well." Squeezing or tampering with skin eruptions has always been discouraged by cosmetologists. But Cayce added "*Provided* the areas are rubbed soon afterwards with this combination:

> 2 oz. Peanut Oil
> 2 oz. Olive Oil
> ¼ oz. Lanolin (Liquefied)   (2072-13)

Peanut oil figures in the treatment of many prominent physical ailments, but in the readings on skin health and beauty peanut oil really shines—perhaps more brightly than other oils—due to its energy-giving qualities: "If they [peanut oil rubs] are taken once a week, it is not too often. For, they do supply energies to the body." (1158-31)

An elderly woman concerned about the texture of her facial skin was told that "the general massage with Peanut Oil will be found to be most beneficial. Take just a small quantity morning and evening and massage the face, neck and shoulders with same, as well as the hands and arms." (2535-1)

Dry skin, a by-product of modern life, was the subject of many appeals for help. "Use the Peanut Oil, as indicated, and we will find this will change the whole condition of the skin in a little while." Then, physically sensing an imminent condition, Cayce further suggested to this particular woman, "Should there become any disturbance or prickling from same, add a small quantity of Lanolin (dissolved)—a teaspoonful, or half a teaspoonful to four ounces." (1770-7)

Skin care advice was not confined to adults. Teenagers—and even those younger—brought Cayce their problems. One eleven-year-old youngster was given advice for improving skin conditions of face, back, scalp and hair. "At least once a week," Cayce outlined, "after a good, thorough workout of the body in exercise—following the bath afterward, massage the back, the face, the body, the limbs with pure Peanut Oil, then this will add to the beauty." Cayce then went on to outline a program which, if followed, could well be considered a life-prolonging formula. "And know, if ye would take each day through thy experience, two almonds, ye will never have skin blemishes, ye will never be tempted ever in body toward cancer nor towards those things that make blemishes in the body forces themselves. And the oil rubs once a week, ye will never have rheumatism nor those concurrent conditions from stalemate in liver and kidney activities." (1206–13)

Peanut oil was often used in conjunction with other oils and ingredients. The following is such a compound:

"To six ounces of Peanut Oil add:
   2 oz. Olive Oil
   2 oz. Rosewater
   1 tbsp. Lanolin (dissolved)"

This was recommended as a massage for making or keeping a good complexion—for the skin, the hands, the arms and the body as well. "This would be used after a tepid bath, in which the body has remained for at least fifteen to twenty minutes; giving the body then a thorough rub with any good soap—to stimulate the body forces . . .

"And afterwards massage this solution, after shaking it well. Of course, this will be sufficient for many times. Shake well and pour in an open saucer or the like; dipping fingers in same. Begin with the face, neck, shoulders, arms; and then the whole body would be massaged thoroughly with the solution; especially in the limbs—in the areas that would come across the hips; across the body, across the diaphragm.

"This will not only keep a stimulating in the body, but will aid in keeping the body beautiful; that is, as to any blemish of any nature." (1968–7)

Though castor oil wasn't mentioned in the readings for cosmetic use, it did appear as a remedy for just about everything else. It is widely accepted as a softening and smoothing agent for the skin. Applied and left on overnight it is a good wrinkle discourager. (Tissue off the excess before getting into bed.)

One top-priced New York dermatologist was in the habit of prescribing a small bottle of castor oil for her patients, to be applied to the under-eye area before retiring. The charge for filling this prescription was usually about five dollars, although the cost of the oil was only nineteen cents. One patient had her son, a pharmacist, fill the prescription and the cat was out of the bag. When confronted by the patient, the dermatologist simply stated that if it were known that the ingredient was pure castor oil, her patients would not be consistent with their use of it, and *how many would expect results?* "Expect much, you will obtain much! Expect little, you will obtain little! Expect nothing, you will obtain nothing!" (5325-1) "For he that expects much—if he lives and uses that in hand day by day—shall be *full* to running over." (557-3)

Packs

Mud packs or masks, as they are more familiarly known today, are usually astringent in action and provide a stimulation to the skin. Their use was suggested in a number of readings given by Cayce for conditions that ranged from sagging facial muscles to providing pleasure.

Q. "How can sagging facial muscles be avoided? How corrected?"

A. "By massage and the use of those creams as indicated (Black and White) . . . occasionally, the use of the Boncilla or need packs would be very good." (1947-4)

For a case where there was the building up of disturbances in the glandular system, Cayce advised: "About twice a month . . . we would have the mud packs; face and neck, across the shoulders and upper portions about the neck; especially extending over the area of the thyroids—as an astringent and as a stimulation for a better circulation throughout the system." (1968-3)

The following provides a clue as to why this particular mud pack was so frequently recommended:

Q. "Is the mud pack I'm using the proper sort?"

A. "As we find, the Boncilla would be more preferable than this, that is, more because of the nature of the chalk that is in same." (1709-5)

A note of human interest very often crept into the readings. One example is Cayce's reply to a woman who asked if she should continue her mud packs. "It would be well occasionally," he conceded, "but not too often," since the other treatments she was taking might soon eliminate the need. Then, almost as though sensing an unspoken disappointment, he added, "Once a month, for the very pleasure of it, we would have the mud pack." (1968-7)

Sunbathing

Careless sunbathing has probably accounted for more prematurely wrinkled and leathery skins than any other single cause. A seldom considered fact is that the same rays that form vitamin D on the skin eventually produce tanning, which itself progressively inhibits vitamin D formation. In other words, the darker the skin becomes, the less vitamin D is formed.

Cayce explained: "It is not well that there be too much tan from the sun on the body. This [tan] forms on the body to protect the body from same [the sun]. Thus not too much tan, but sufficient for the healthy activity of the body." (3172-2)

It is not necessary to tan in order to benefit from the sun. Sunbathing in the shade permits the body to receive reflected doses of health-giving vitamin D without the undesirable side-effects of the sun (sunburn, sunstroke, peeling, etc.) But if we must sunbathe: "Let there not be too much activity in the middle of the day, or too *much* of the sunshine. The early mornings and the late afternoons are the preferable times. For the sun—during the period between eleven or eleven-thirty and two o'clock—carries too great a quantity of the actinic rays that make for destructive forces to the superficial circulation." (934-2)

In a reading for a child Cayce advised the mother to give the child a sunbath but ". . . never during the period from eleven to two P.M.—then the body should not be in the sun." (3172-2)

In effect, the readings seemed to agree that sunbathing was fine—in moderation.

"Sunbaths are of benefit to MOST bodies; would be helpful to this [body] if not too *much* is given—for it enlivens the capillary circulation . . ."

Q. "About how long at a time?"
A. "Twenty to thirty minutes. NOT LONGER."

Q. "Each day?"
A. "Each day." (5455-1)

SUMMARY

I. Soaps
Use Castile or pure soap with olive oil or coconut oil base.

II. Creams

A. Alkaline only. Use no preparations carrying lead. Alkalinity can be tested with Nitrazine paper.
B. Use no deodorants.

III. Oils and fresheners for use after cleansing the skin

A. For all skins, dry or oily, use:
   8 oz. olive oil
   1 oz. rosewater
   few drops glycerine
   1 oz. 10 percent solution of alcohol
B. For skin suffering from eruptions, use:
   2 parts camphorated oil
   1 part witch hazel
   1 part Russian white oil

Shake well before using.

IV. Packs

A. Mud packs, or masks, to be used for sagging facial muscles.
B. Mud packs may also be used for stimulation and better circulation throughout system.

V. Sunbathing

Never sunbathe between 11:00 A.M and 2:00 P.M.

CHAPTER 3

Exterior Flaws and Their Remedies

SOME SKIN PROBLEMS:
EPIDERMAL POLTERGEIST

Acne, Psoriasis and Herpes Simplex

IN ATTEMPTING an analysis of skin problems, passages have been selected from the many readings given for acne—probably the most common skin problem—and for psoriasis and herpes simplex, commonly known as the cold sore or fever blister, both of which are too common today. If these causes and cures are studied, it might give us a clearer insight into 'why' and 'how' the manifestations appear on the skin's surface to torment teenagers and embarrass adults.

When giving a physical reading, the sleeping Cayce would first, in the body of the reading, examine the blood, nervous system, glandular imbalance—if any—and eliminations, coordinations and assimilations. He would then give advice on the corrections of any of the disturbances in the body. It was interesting to note, while researching the readings, that many of the external lotions and 'beauty' preparations were requested in the question and answer period immediately after the bulk of the reading had been given. It was as though something as frivolous as this was

not considered important enough to offer voluntarily. It was
hardly ever refused, for Edgar Cayce was very gracious—most of
the time—when in trance. After giving the treasured formula
as a kind of bonus, he would usually add that when the internal
conditions were attended to, the external manifestations would
disappear by themselves.

Dr. William McGarey, M.D. states in his commentary on acne
that,—according to Edgar Cayce—"Acne is . . . a chronic inflammatory disease of the sebaceous glands, occurring most frequently
on the face, back and chest. The basic physiological malfunction
occurring in the body which gives rise to acne is an imbalance
of the eliminating systems of the body, although there are several
mechanisms that can play a part in the production of this imbalance."*

When speaking of eliminations, most people think only of
the bowels. But when Edgar Cayce spoke of eliminations, he
was referring to all the organs involved: alimentary canal, kidneys, respiratory and perspiratory systems, plus all other bodily
activities to which these give rise in a chain reaction.

Dr. McGarey continues, "Some of the factors causing the elimination imbalance are incoordination between the deep and
superficial circulation; improper diet during the period of men-
arche (beginning of menses); nervous tensions and suppressions
of fears; and glandular reactions and the gradual building of difficulties related to the glands and circulation."**

The following 'no-nonsense' answers, short and sweet, must
make clear Cayce's instructions for the first step to a healthy
skin:

Q. What can be done locally for impurities on face?

A. "Keep the eliminations open." (452–2)

---

* From the *Physician's Reference Notebook*, available to cooperating physicians and in the circulating file of the Association for Research and Enlightenment, available to ARE members.
** Ibid.

Q. How can the body clear up the complexion?

A. "Correcting eliminations, as given." (1816–3)

Q. What is still causing my face and neck to break out in pimples and what can be done to cure them completely?

A. "These will disappear if the corrections are made properly and the eliminations are kept well." (3081–3)

Q How may I best clear up my complexion?

A. "By increasing or stimulating the general circulation for coordination in the eliminations." (1101–4)

Q. Can anything be done for pimples and breaking out of the skin?

A. "The exercise and the diets are better than lotions and applications, see?" (1771–3)

Q. What is the cause of my skin eruptions that I have so frequently, and kindly give me a cure for same.

A. "These are part of the circulatory disturbance, and as the eliminations are set up and as there are coordinations between the forces in the body itself that make for a coordinant reaction in all portions of the eliminations, we will find these disturbances being eliminated." (603–3)

As a final driving home of the point, 1993–1 said that her face had cleared in the past week and asked, "Is this due to any particular treatment or environment?" Cayce answered that ". . . there are periods when this will clear to a great degree; but the *sources* of the disturbance must be eliminated, see?" He was truly a perfectionist.

The information 528–2 received was unique in the nearly fifteen thousand readings which were given: "For the exterior forces where abrasions have left effects, especially for the time of the scar tissue, where the eruptions show, we find that it would be most helpful at first—when the tissue forms into eruptions and collects (the matter in same)—open these places with potsherd (pottery) or glass; which would be much better than any prick or the like, and will cleanse the skin more thoroughly."

Frightening as this may sound, the method of treatment is far from new. In the book of Job (2:7-8) we find: "So went Satan forth from the presence of the Lord, and smote Job with sore boils from the sole of his foot unto his crown. And he took him a potsherd to scrape himself withal . . ."

One might wonder what comments today's dermatologists might have concerning this, and above all what degree and type of pustular infection would warrant the use of this method of cleansing. Cayce then advised following this cleansing with the skin clearing compound mentioned in Chapter 2, page 31. He claimed that this would prevent scarring.

The same young lady was told that ". . . When using the powder for face (as blotches on face), only use the pure talcum with Stearate and Balsam of Tolu in same; that is the balsam and stearate and *pure* talcum *as* a powder. None of those that have been highly scented with other ingredients."

More about acne in future chapters on eliminations and diet and exercise.

Case 5152-1 concerns a young lady of twenty-six who had been suffering for a year with herpes simplex. She had been to the Mayo Brothers' Clinic and to two other specialists, who all agreed that she would 'probably' get well, but did not offer to say when (according to her mother's letter to Edgar Cayce).

Herpes simplex is a growing problem today. Once someone is afflicted with a cold sore or fever blister, it usually keeps returning. How often and what triggers its return may vary with each person. Sometimes a day in the sun might be the start of one, and here we can remember Cayce's warning that sunbathing between the hours of eleven-thirty and two o'clock may be destructive to superficial circulation (see chapter 2, page 36).

It was found that 5152-1's trouble resulted from ". . . the great amount of acidity in the system and the tendency for the use (or the necessity for the use of that) for the greater eliminations through the alimentary canal. These are the sources or causes of this. As we find here, it will require patience, persistence, if we would eliminate this character of acidity from the system.

"As we would find, we would begin and take at least three or five glasses of water, carrying Glyco-Thymoline. This is not all the water to be taken. Drink about six or eight glasses of water daily, but in at least three of these, put five drops of Glyco-Thymoline.

"Also we would have colonic irrigations to eliminate the sedatives which would have been parts of the consciousness through the activity, or lack of activity, in the gall duct area, so as to make proper coordination between the general conditions which exist through the body.

"We would do these, and use over the abdominal area, as well as the area along the right side, Glyco-Thymoline packs. These we would do regularly. Do this about two days in succession and rest a period of two days between each series. These should be taken for AT LEAST one hour. Saturate cotton cloth, three to four thicknesses, with Glyco-Thymoline.

"Do this and keep the diet towards those things that produce eliminations."

Why the packs? Glyco-Thymoline is an anti-mucous solution —among other things. Herpes simplex are also known as cold sores. The following was given as an explanation of the action of the Glyco-Thymoline pack: "The oils in this (Glyco-Thymoline) as well as the tendency for the relaxing of the tissue through the body, will produce therapeutic reaction not only in the body forces, where atrophied conditions tend to be, but will relieve the tensions also and produce activities." (3045-1)

The colonics were to eliminate the "sedatives which have been parts of the consciousness." What had Cayce to say of sedatives? "A bromide of any nature *must* eventually become destructive to the physical forces of a body; a hypnotic of any nature, if continued to be used must become destructive to the better functioning of the body." (1264–1) And furthermore "Sedatives and hypnotics are destructive forces to brain and nerve reflexes." (3431–1) Please note that there was nothing suggested for external use at all.

Psoriasis is a chronic disease in which the patient is haunted by red, dry, scaly lesions on the skin. These are frequently to be found on the scalp, knees or elbows, but may involve almost any area of the skin's surface.

To quote Fred D. Lansford, Jr., M.D., "The readings have rather specific things to say regarding the pathological process commonly known as psoriasis. In reading after reading it is mentioned that the diseased state of the skin and joint tissues is due to a thinning of the walls of the intestinal tract. In most cases the readings specify the jejunum as the site of the intestinal lesion although the lower portion of the duodenum is also quite often mentioned. This thinning of the intestinal walls then allows toxic products from the intestinal tract to leak into the circulatory system and find their way into the lymph flow of the skin. When the blood and lymph systems of the body are unable to eliminate these poisons, then the inflammatory skin reaction known as psoriasis is produced." *

Q. "Is psoriasis always from the same cause?"

A. "No, but it is more often from the lack of proper coordination in the eliminating systems. At times the pressures may be in those areas disturbing the equilibrium between the heart and liver, or between heart and lungs. BUT IT IS ALWAYS CAUSED BY A CONDITION OF A LACK OF LYMPH CIRCULATION THROUUGH ALIMENTARY CANAL AND BY ABSORPTION OF SUCH ACTIVITIES THROUGH THE BODY." (5016–1)

* From the *Physician's Reference Notebook* and ARE Circulating File.

Although the initial contributory causes may differ, the final cause is essentially the same.

To treat psoriasis then, anti-itch ointments may act as a temporary palliative, but for permanent relief, the body would have to be rid of the circulating poisons and the lesions healed, while improving the coordination between the organ systems.

The various treatments which Edgar Cayce gave toward this end were diet, eliminations, osteopathic manipulations and other physio-therapeutic measures to relieve pressures where necessary and improve circulation, and some herbals to promote healing of the lesions.

The diet: "Stress seafoods and fowl. Little of beef or other meats. Use at least three vegetables that grow above the ground to one that grows under the ground, and we will find better conditions for this body." (3373–1) "Eliminate fats, sweets and pastries from the diet. DO have a great deal of fruits and vegetables." (5016–1)

When asked about alcoholic beverages, he answered 745–1, "Wines; but not the stronger drinks—not rum or the like."

The eliminations: "BE SURE THERE ARE THE FULL ELIMINATIONS THROUGH THE ALIMENTARY CANAL EACH DAY . . ." (641–5)

This gives the lie to the theory of some that each system acts differently and that it doesn't matter if a day or two or three are missed here and there without having an elimination.

When asked about eliminants, he answered the same man in another reading: "This depends upon the eliminations. Be sure there is one or two good evacuations each day." (641–7)

The herbals: "Then begin with Yellow Saffron tea, a pinch of the American Saffron in a cup of boiling water—or put in a cup and fill with boiling water, allow to stand for thirty minutes, strain and drink, each evening when ready to retire.

"Occasionally, about two or three times a week, drink Elm Water—a pinch of ground Elm (between thumb and forefinger) in a cup filled with warm water (not boiling water). Stir thoroughly and let set for thirty minutes. Drink this preferably of morning rather than at the period when Saffron Tea is taken." (5016–1)

It is also interesting to note that the same herbals were given as one specific in treatments for stomach ulcers.

Case 745–1 was also told to take small internal doses of olive oil, ½ to ¼ teaspoonful every three or four hours during the waking period but cyclically, for three or four days, then leave off for three or four days. The following reading may cast some light on this subject: cyclic doses of *anything*.

"Take periods of [specific medication]; not continued every day but for a week every day, rest a week and begin again. These are more effective than (if) continued, for ANY property. For this may be said to be the manner in which outside influence acts upon not only this body, but ANY body.

"To continue the use of any one influence that is active upon the body continually is to cause those portions of the system that produce same to lose their activity or their significance, and depend upon the supply from without.

"But to give stimulation to the system and then refrain from same tends to produce in the body that necessary reaction in the glandular system and in the functioning of the organs. For the body [normal] produces within itself the necessary elements for its continual reproduction of itself at all times." (1100–8)

A reliance on daily doses of anything—whether laxatives, antacids or vitamin pills—inhibits the natural functions of the body's mechanisms and denies its full potential.

Are we going to approach with new understanding these manifestations which appear on the skin as having a deeper cause, or are we still going to be searching for the magic lotion?

Blackheads

Case 1101–3 asked about warts. Cayce told her exactly how to treat them, explaining that "these [warts] are as but those eliminations in system being thrown out in improper directions" and went on to tackle another facet of these misdirected eliminations: "As is seen also from pores that appear to be large, or blackheads, or spots appearing in portions of the skin . . .

"Then for these on face and neck—well that there be made local application first of a warm Turkish towel; not hot, not steaming, but warm Turkish towel, wet, and let it remain for eight to ten minutes. Then rub thoroughly with pure Castile Soap. Then put on *cold* cloths for one to two minutes, until three or four are applied. Then *pat* the skin very thoroughly with the hands, until the circulation in the face and neck is thoroughly established again. Do not use creams or face powders while this is being applied, that will fill up the pores again. If there is the necessity for making the skin more smooth, then use Magnesia —or Cornstarch *and* Magnesia, which is the better for ANY skin . . ."

Q. "Is there not a treatment or method that might be used for the removal of blackheads from the face?"

A. "The general building up of the body forces and the establishing first of correct coordination of eliminations. These will gradually be removed.

"There might be used bleaches, or cleansing creams, but these would eventually give more trouble than the blackheads are causing in the present. Get to the basic condition of these . . . (2072-9)

Freckles
Freckles seem to skip in and out of fashion. Just a short while ago, one of France's leading couturiers instructed his models to apply freckles with a light brown eyebrow pencil. It seems that in Cayce's time, many of his clients wanted to know how to get *rid* of them. His replies were basically the same. Here are a few examples:

Q. "What causes moles, pigments and freckles?"

A. "Get rid of these by creating better eliminations and normal

coordination between all of the organs of eliminations; alimentary canal, kidneys, lungs, respiratory and perspiratory systems."
(5271–1)

Q. "What is the best treatment for freckles?"

A. "You'd better try and keep your freckles and not try to get
rid of them . . . these are in the pigment of the skin, and unless
you wish to upset something else, don't attempt to bleach more
than you would have from the regular condition. These are
partially liver conditions but don't be touchy about freckles,
they're good for you. (5223–1)

Q. "What can be done to get rid of freckles?"

A. "You'd better try to keep 'em, than trying to bleach or use
any of the conditions!"
The correction of the diets, though, should change these, so
that what is the better for the body will be the regular reaction
to same." (1431–2)

He was not *always* so adamant about changing from within
without any external forces. When 301–8 asked, "What is the
best way of removing freckles?" he told her: "A combination of
Wheat Bran made with any good cleansing cream or soap will
remove freckles; that is, of a general nature.

"This is made [Whole Wheat Bran] with warm water, that
makes sort of a mush, see? After the use of same, cleanse with
any good soap."

Birthmarks
Have you ever wondered why some people have marks on their
bodies? 540–3 did and asked Cayce, "Why do I have a mark
on my physical body?" She was told: "There is set a mark in
those that they-themselves may know that they have been called;
that they may understand that they have been called. For it
has been given, 'I will set my mark upon my own, and they shall
hear My voice, and answer—within.' Seek into self to know

where unto such has called thee, that ye answer, even as HE, 'Here am I, Lord, use me as thou seest fit.' "

One young mother, 573–1, was concerned about her baby and asked what caused the birthmark on its arm and how to remove it. She was told: "By massaging it with an equal mixture of Olive Oil and Castor Oil—it will be prevented from increasing.

"Marks on bodies, as on this one, are for a purpose—and if a life reading would be given it would be seen that it (the child) has a purpose to perform in the affairs of those in its own surroundings and in many others. A mark!"

Warts

The most common occurrence of warts seems to be just before puberty and in the teen years. When a twelve year old asked what causes warts, she was told that "This is a period of transition and these are the results of the cellular force changing—which comes to every individual through those periods of transition." (1206–6)

Another was told: "It is the accumulation of cellular forces attempting to act themselves. Or as we see, every atom of the body is as a whole universe or an element in itself. It either coordinates or makes for disruptive forces by its activity being expelled from the system, through the activity of the eliminating system; and as it accumulates it gathers those things about it and is not absorbed. Hence we have them as moles or warts." (759–9)

Warts, also known as verrucae, have plagued mankind for centuries. Very few people escape without ever having experienced a wart. The *National Disease and Therapeutic Index*, which is a medical publication, reports that in 1969, 5.5 million visits were made to physicians for wart treatment. This is 20 percent more than in 1965.

Cures for warts have been sought through the years with varied findings and success. One seventeenth-century English nobleman claimed that he cured *his* warts by washing his hands in moonbeams. Gypsies rub their warts on the back of the father of an illegitimate child. Moroccans have a special saint to whom they pray for the removal of warts. Others have tried tobacco juice, axle grease and morning dew. More recently, warts have been cauterized, frozen, bombarded with X-rays and swabbed with acid. However, modern medicine uses curettage, or surgical removal; fulguration and electrodesication, which are two means of destroying warts by the use of high frequency electrical sparks; and chemotherapy.

Although most warts are harmless, a cure for them has long eluded the medical profession. Dr. John Gowdy, Medical Services Director of the Bureau of Drugs, says that one form of cancer looks like a wart. Carl Abramson, Director of Basic Science at Pennsylvania College of Podiatric Medicine in Philadelphia, who is conducting one of the few wart-study programs in the nation, believes that wart research may provide a clue to a cure for cancer.

Case 583-7 asked, "Has the body a tendency toward cancer? If not, why the disturbance and itching of moles and beauty spots at times?" She was told: "The conditions as are produced about such spots are more from poor eliminations as are shown in the body and the nerve reaction as is seen, than that of the tendency towards cancerous condition—for, as we have given, cancerous conditions are where cellular forces have congregated on account of irritation, or poor elimination and irritation following, and the system attempting to relieve same sets up from broken cellular tissue the condition from within which becomes malignant . . . in this body, there is not an indication at present of any malignant serum or tissue in the body. There are indications of poor eliminations and misdirected nerve tissue, see?"

To return to warts, 759-9 asked: "What will eliminate the warts from hand and body?" and was told to "Massage them with Castor Oil." She then asked "how often?" and was told: "Every evening." Then she wanted to know when she could expect results from this treatment for the warts, and was told, "In two or three weeks."

Q. "The small growth on the first finger of my right hand is still there. Should anything further be done?"

A. "This may be massaged with pure Castor Oil and be removed, see?"

Q. "How often?"

A. "About twice a day; before retiring and when arising." (261–10)

Q. "What can I do for a crown of warts under right thumb-nail?"

A. "Where those blemishes are indicated on thumb and on parts of the body, as they occur, use Baking Soda combined with Castor Oil—made into an ointment and bound on. This will make it very sore for a day, and then take off the binding but massage it with this mixture every other day—and it will disappear." (3414–1)

Q. "What can be done to cure warts?"

A. "These may be treated by the use of an application of nitrate; or preferably, as we find, the use of the soda with Castor Oil. Not made to be as dough, but as putty or soft putty—this put on, and we will find them disappearing." (1206–5)

Q. "How to get rid of warts?"

A. "Apply a paste of Baking Soda with Castor Oil. Mix together and apply of evening. Just the proportions so it makes almost a gum; not as dough, but more as gum, see? A pinch between the fingers with three or four drops in the palm of the hand, and this worked together and then placed on—bound on. It may make for irritation after the second or third application but leave it off for one evening and then apply the next—and it will be disappearing." (1179–3)

Q. "What is the best way to remove warts?"

A. "This one on the right knee is gradually leaving. Put equal portions of Castor Oil and Soda on the fingertip, massage this, it'll make it sore but it'll take it away also." (308–13)

Q. "How can I remove the knot on my right second finger?" (This sounds like a common place: the pressure point from holding a writing instrument.)

A. "Massage with Castor Oil and Soda mixed." (303–32)

Q. "Can anything be done to remove small wart-like growth on right knee which lately is beginning to grow and spread?"

A. "Massage with mixing Camphor and Soda, it'll make it awful sore after the second or third day, but it will disappear." (5290–1)

About sixteen years after this reading was given for 5290-1, she wrote to ARE to report that she used this formula on her daughter's thumb, alongside which there were eight warts. After just a few applications the warts dissolved and now her "thumb is perfectly clean."

There are many letters in the files attesting to the success of treatments given for warts, moles and cysts. Not all were given for the patient as the above case testifies. Many letters are from recent ARE members who have seen the readings and have in desperation tried these remedies . . . with success.

There are a couple of cases where hydrochloric acid, 20 percent solution, was advised. "In touching them with the acid, it is preferable to use either a glass pestle [that is, a small round piece of glass] or a broomstraw. But," Cayce warned, "Do not pick at them as the discoloration takes place, and as they begin to deteriorate!" (487–22)

Case 274 was told that C. P. Hydrochloric solution, 20 percent, will remove these if it is applied sufficiently often: "Not so as to produce irritation, but often enough that it may *destroy* the tendencies for the broken cells (of which warts are formed) to make or form accumulations." (274–6)

Case 2803-5 was told: "Wash these occasionally in a solution of alum water. Take a piece of alum about the size of a partridge egg and rinse it in rather warm water, but not hot, tepid, then rinse the hands in this, allowing it to dry on them."

Doctors agree that by far the most difficult warts to treat and cure are planter's warts which appear on the soles of the feet and around finger nails. Cayce gave a simple remedy.

Q. "There are two growths that appear to be warts on the ball of my left foot; what is the best way to dissolve them or remove them?"

A. "Apply each evening a small amount of Baking Soda wet thoroughly with Spirits Of Camphor or, just sufficient to cover same—and bind on so as to keep over the night. This will cause some little sharp pain, and a little soreness for a few days, but it will dissolve and prevent any irritation following same; for these are as but those eliminations in system being thrown out in improper directions." (1101-3)

Cayce then goes on, without further questions, "As is seen also from pores that appear to be large, or blackheads, or spots appearing in portions of the skin." He then continues with a complete rundown of a routine to eliminate the cause.

Moles
Is a pattern beginning to emerge from these readings for you? Let us go onto the mole, close relative of the wart.

Q. "How may the moles be removed from the body?"

A. "Don't worry about those! Worry more about correcting the internal forces, and let these take care of themselves! These are usually as signs." (361-3)

Q. "What should I do about the mole on my neck, on which the doctor put some acid for removal?"

A. "Not anything in the present. As those properties suggested begin to take effect, and there are the adjustments in the circulation, we find these will gradually take away the conditions.

"We would keep same soft with a little of an equal combination of Mutton Tallow (melted), Spirits of Camphor and Spirits of Turpentine; not so much put on the area of the mole itself as the area about it, so that it will be absorbed by the effects of the properties through the radiation, see?" (2426-1)

Q. "Is the mole over liver malignant? and what must I do for it?"

A. "This as we find is not malignant. While the conditions of the body do not permit of the body's undergoing an anaesthesia for the removal, this might be done by local anaesthesia or local application—if it is chosen by the body to be removed.

"For if it is tampered with, by rubbings or the applications that cause a growth, it may become so deep-seated as to cause a great deal more disturbance.

"But the better way is to use the application of those things that make for the retarding of its growth; as the combination of equal portions Mutton Suet, Turpentine and Camphor—not upon the area itself but the surrounding area, or surrounding portions. This, gently massaged, will tend to retard or keep down irritation and retard any tendency for growth; and gradually make for easing. Yet it may be removed by operative measures if so chosen—or if it becomes too much inflamed. Otherwise we would leave it as it is, using those conditions as indicated." (1010-11)

It seems that moles should not be taken too lightly.

Q. "Should moles on the back be removed? If so, by whom, and what method?"

A. "As we find, these are not to be disturbed to the extent of any material or outside influence. The massaging of same (by self, or one who may do same for the body) with just the Castor Oil will prevent growth—and, if persistent with same (not bruising same)—it will remove same entirely." (678-2)

Here once again the key is 'persistence' and once again castor oil is called into play. Castor oil, otherwise known as the Palma Christi, or the hand of Christ, seems to be a wonder. The full scope of its potential has yet to be determined.

Q. "What treatment would remove the mole on my chest, or is this advisable?" asked 573-1 on June 6, 1934.

A. ". . . the massage with the Castor Oil twice each day; not rubbing hard, but *gentle* massage around and over this place and it will be removed."

On March 9, 1935, it was reported that the mole had entirely disappeared.

Reports have also been received that castor oil applications gradually get rid of those brown spots sometimes referred to as 'liver spots' or 'old-age marks.'

Here is a wonderful example of Edgar Cayce's "do what is at hand" attitude, or first things first:

Q. "What is the cause and cure for the mole on my forehead?"

A. "This is a pressure of a cell that broke, caused from the time of some activities in the growing of the body itself. Do not let this disturb thee at present. Later we will make application of a gentle massage of Castor Oil and overcome much of it. But we must make the proper assimilations and the proper activity of the respiratory system before we commence troubling with this." (626-1)

Q. "What should be done for the small mole or soft growth on left side of back?"

A. "Use a small quantity of Castor Oil with a little Soda mixed in same. This will make it sore for a day or two, then it will disappear.

Q. "Just rub it on?"

A. "Just rub it on, two or three days apart, for two or three times." (4033-2)

This particular mole appears to be "not so delicate as the others" and a soda mixture is called for. It seems that the more delicate the mole, the less stringent the treatment. In some cases, the *building up of the body forces is first advised*. At other times, gentle massage around the area, to prevent growth. Then castor oil is recommended to be rubbed around, and, almost as an afterthought, over the area. Yet again he cautions *gentle* massage and even mentions "not bruising same." Moles require a great deal of careful treatment.

Another relative, or maybe ancestor, of the mole made its appearance on case 288-51. It was described as a "blistered freckle caused by over-exposure to the sun."

"This is from a broken cell. Do not irritate too much, or this may turn into a mole or wart—which would be a disfiguration to the body.

"We would keep a little Camphor or Camphorice on same of evenings."

The follow-up reading advised the continued use of camphor. Nearly a year later she reported that "the red spot on my nose has been completely absorbed and eliminated, by using the Spirits of Camphor each evening as suggested."

The following casts some light on moles from yet another angle, from the same inquirer:

Q. "The numerous moles which continue to occur, especially on upper part of body?"

A. "This is mostly the imagination, for they come and go. And if there is kept good eliminations, we will find these will not appear."

Case 3607–2, when asking why the spot "on side doesn't clear up" was given an answer which might apply to any trouble, for anybody. "Don't be impatient. Did it grow in a day? Don't expect it to be eliminated in a day or a month. It took years to grow and it will require several months to disappear. But it will be eliminated if we follow through. IT IS JUST AS BAD TO OVERDO IN TAKING THE MEDICINES AS IT IS TO UNDERDO. Do as given . . ."

The same advice was given in a slightly different way to case 1861–11: "As to the application [of specific treatment], there has been indicated a specific time. This has been overstepped at times, with the idea that if a little would do good, more would do more good; while at times does harm rather than good!

"It is as an overtaxation even to a strong muscular force. May weaken, may even deter the best activity. Do not overstrain but keep the [specific treatment] and not more than the minute or minute and a half. Two or three minutes is worse than none being given!"

Scars

Experience has shown that often where a scar is present, so is embarrassment and self-consciousness. More people are concerned with covering scars and self-decreed imperfections than with underlining good features, which, if played up, would often create a trompe l'oeil and draw attention away from the offending area. Play up the good features, and the bad just disappear of their own accord.

On October 11, 1940, Mr. Cayce received a frantic phone call at his home. A one-year-old child (a girl) had accidentally pulled over a pan of boiling water onto her face, stomach and feet—all burned very badly. Her doctor thought that one eye was burned. Cayce started the reading: "Yes—we have the body here . . . While these appear very serious in the present, because of the blisters or the water, we do not find the injury to the eyes, but rather to the lids.

"As we find, we would cleanse and use the tannic acid; followed with the Unguentine and the Sweet Oil, camphorated to prevent or remove scars, as the tissue heals." (2015-6)

Shakespeare stated that it is an ill wind which blows no good. This child's burns were completely healed and the formula which Cayce gave in a follow-up reading for her has become the classic 'Cayce Scar Formula,' a remedy used with success by thousands since it was first given.

Q. "Will the continued use of Camphorice gradually eliminate scar on arm [resulting from severe burn two years ago]?"

A. "Camphorice, or better—as we find—Camphorated Oil. Or make thine own Camphorated Oil; that is, by taking the regular Camphorated Oil and adding to it; in these proportions:

    2 oz. Camphorated Oil
    ½ tsp. Lanolin, dissolved
    1 oz. Peanut Oil

This combination will quickly remove this tendency of the scar —or scar tissue."

It was reported to an ARE Congress in June of 1963 that a young lady from Ohio had used the formula to prevent her brother-in-law's acid burns from scarring. Unexpectedly, the formula burned so that the original burn was intensified. Upon inquiring of the druggist who had prepared it, it was found that instead of using the olive oil base (or as it is also called, Sweet Oil) in the camphorated oil, as *specified in the readings,* cottonseed oil was used as an equivalent, as is still the custom. As soon as the formulation was changed to comply with Cayce's specifications, the applications did *not* burn and scarring *was* prevented.

Case 440-3's reading was quoted earlier stating that "Olive Oil is one of the most effective agents for stimulating muscular activity that may be applied to a body. . . ."

The same reading continues: "Camphorated Oil is merely the same basic force (Olive Oil) to which has been added properties of Camphor in more or less its raw state than the spirits of same. Such activity in the epidermis is not only to produce soothing to the affected area, but to stimulate the circulation in such effectual ways and manners as to combine with the other properties in bringing what will be determined, in the course of two to two and a half years, a new skin."

With a promise like that, one can learn to exercise patience and do whatever must be done.

The following excerpt from a letter to Hugh Lynn Cayce is from a physician and surgeon from Kansas City, Missouri, and is dated April 6, 1959:

"I spoke to you about using the scar lotion which I obtained from the personal file of your father's readings. We are pleased to report that it was most helpful in helping my daughter, who had a keloid on her wrist following a severe cut on a glass window pane. The keloid was removed surgically once. It returned twice as big, and was removed by surgical planing. It again returned. I used the scar lotion coupled with Ultra Sound applications. I am glad to report that the keloid has disappeared, not only that, but it takes close scrutiny to determine its original location. We have been so impressed with this lotion that in ninety percent of our surgeries, it is now used in the post-surgical care phase.

"Another case that you may be interested in is a four-year-old girl who was run over by a truck, fracturing both femurs. The right femur was corrected by open reduction. The scar lotion was used on the incision area. This past summer found the scar tissue soft and flush with the surrounding tissue. The scar had also taken on pigmentation and tanned at the same rate and degree as the surrounding skin."

(signed) Dr. J. L. Rowland D.O., MSPH, FAPHA

A seventeen-year-old girl (475-1) asked:

Q. "Will this treatment relieve the condition without leaving scars [acne]?"

A. "As there is the tendency for the stopping of accumulations in the skin, it would be well to massage these portions with Camphorated Oil, as this will tend to soften the skin and aid in keeping scar tissue from forming, not too often, but when ready for retiring, massage gently over those portions affected. Camphorated Oil. But we would add the other things as suggested." (Diet, X Ray, Physiotherapy, internal doses of Olive Oil and Saffron tea etc.)

For a fifty-two-year-old man, he said: "Use any character of ointment, preferably though, we would suggest Cocoa Butter that is dissolved or rubbed in with Olive Oil; as this will aid in preventing scars, even upon the areas where old sores and injuries have been so disturbing to the body." (2423-1)

Many readings contain tincture of myrrh in their formulas for skin care or therapy. About tincture of myrrh: ". . . acts with the pores of the skin in such a manner as to strike in, causing the circulation to be carried to affected parts [scars]. . . ." (440-3)

The same gentleman asked if the scars on his legs or stomach were in any way detrimental to the proper functioning of his body. He was told:

"Little or no hindrance. These may be aided in being removed by sufficient time, precaution and persistence in activity; by the massage over those portions of small quantities at a time of Tincture of Myrrh and Olive Oil and Camphorated Oil. These would be massaged at different times to be sure, one one day, and one the second day from same—see? In preparing the Olive Oil and Tincture of Myrrh, heat the oil and add the Myrrh—equal portions, only preparing such quantity as would be used at each application.* The Camphorated Oil may be obtained in quantity. Only massage such quantities as the cuticle and epidermis will absorb. This will require, to be sure, a long period, but remember *the whole surface may be entirely changed* if this is done persistently and consistently. In the massaging, do not

---

* Author's note: Remove olive oil from heat before adding the myrrh, as the latter is highly volatile.

massage so roughly as to produce irritation. The properties are to be absorbed. Do not merely pat the solution on but do not use tufts of cotton or other properties to dab it on; dip the fingertips into the solution, and it won't hurt the fingers either—it'll be good for them!—and massage into affected portions."

Much has been said by Cayce on consistency and persistency. So much so in fact that a treatise was done on just that subject.**

He applied it to every facet of living.

One reference to scars is truly worthy of study: "Let the scars be removed from the OWN MENTAL AND SPIRITUAL SELF. Turn to those things of making application of the fruits of the spirit of truth, love, patience, gentleness, kindliness, long suffering, brotherly love, putting away those little tendencies for being 'catty' at times or being selfish or expressing jealousy and such. Let the mind be in thee as was in Him who is the way, the truth and the light, and He will make the light of love so shine through thy countenance that few, if any, will ever see the scars made by self-indulgence in other experiences." (5092–1)

SUMMARY

I. Acne, psoriasis and herpes simplex

A. When skin is troubled watch the eliminatory system carefully.

B. Use no make-ups that are too astringent.

C. Use no highly scented face powders.

D. Watch diet as outlined.

E. Above all, do not seek an external panacea. Seek the cause of the disturbance and balance all facets of natural living habits.

** IRF Supplement, available to members of ARE.

II. Blackheads

A. Apply warm Turkish towel to face.
B. Next, apply Castile soap.
C. Then, apply cold cloths.

III. Freckles

A. May get rid of them with better eliminations.
B. Do not bleach them, however. In any case, it is not necessary to get rid of them.

IV. Birthmarks

A. Birthmarks are for a purpose, which is not always known to us.
B. If you wish, however, you may massage them with a mixture of olive oil and castor oil.

V. Warts

A. Castor oil applied twice daily.
B. For more persistent warts, apply a mixture of castor oil and baking soda.
C. For planters warts use baking soda moistened with spirits of camphor applied twice a day.

VI. Moles

Applications of castor oil, or, better still, no treatment at all.

VII. Scars

Massage with a solution of:

2 oz. camphorated olive oil
1 oz. peanut oil
½ tsp. lanolin (dissolved)

CHAPTER *4* *The Supporting Cast*

FOCUS ON THE EYES, TEETH,
HANDS AND NAILS, FEET

Eyes
OF THE five senses of man, more is learned through that of sight
than of any other. Even when we are not consciously studying,
we are observing. Plotinus stated that the eye would not be able
to see the sun if it were not "a sun itself." The sun is the source
of light—which brought order out of chaos. It is a symbol for
intelligence and spirit. Jesus said that there are none so blind
as those who will not see. Seeing, then, is not always visual.
Experiments are being made both in America and most extensively in Russia with 'sightless vision'. It has been discovered
that both blind and sighted people, when gifted this way, can
actually run their fingers across a flat page and 'see' with their
fingertips what is on the page; some can also tell color.
   The eyes may be our tools for sensing and perceiving that
which is outside of ourselves, but how often they project us to
the outside world. How many times have we heard that the
eyes are the windows of the soul? What does it mean?
   "What then, the entity asks, *is* a soul? What does it look like?

What is its plane of experience or activity? How may ye find one? It may not be separated in a material world from its own place of abode in the body physical, *yet the soul looks through the eyes of a body*—it handles with the emotions of the sense of touch—it may be aware through the factors in every sense, and thus add to its body as much as the food of the material world has made for a growing physical body in which the soul may and does indeed dwell in its passage or activity in any individual phase of an experience in the earth." (487–17)

Seeing, then, with its companion senses, feeds our soul-body as physical food feeds our physical-body. "For the light of the eyes rejoiceth the heart." (Proverbs 15:30.)

Why is it, when we speak to another, we always look into his or her eyes? An averted gaze instinctively arouses suspicion. Let us look visual problems straight in the eye.

Many times, the pressures which caused disturbance to the eyes were pinpointed to the cervical and upper dorsal areas of the spine. "To reach the seat of the trouble [in the focal plane of vision] remove first the cause. We find that this is an impingement of the nerve branch in the second cervical and third dorsal . . . release these nerve centers through osteopathic or chiropractic adjustments." (341–1)

Case 749–1 wanted to know "the condition of the eyes and what would be recommended for treatment?" Cayce answered, "As we find, when the circulations are stimulated especially in the upper dorsal and through cervical areas, these would be materially aided . . ." He did not recommend any other treatment at this time as "Nature—or the body building forces—would be greater corrective influence."

Case 340–23 was troubled with granulated eyelids and wanted to know what caused them. She was given: "The general nervous condition of the body . . . the manipulations—if properly administered through the neck and upper dorsal—will relieve these conditions, and the irritation will gradually disappear. Nervousness!"

Later, in a subsequent reading, she was told to make local application. "To the eyes (because of the irritation of the lids) we would use the scraped Irish potato; using a good antiseptic to bathe same off when the compact of the potato is removed."

Case 409-22 also had granulated lids; she asked what to do for them, and was told: "Use a weak solution of Boracic Acid. About twice each week use also those poultices of scraped Irish potato, bound of an evening over the eye."

This was a remedy often given; in some readings it was stipulated that the potato had to be one from the year before, not sprouted. Case 243-11 had a blur over her eyes and was told that "It would be well that occasionally, once or twice each week, before retiring—apply a poultice of OLD Irish potato, well scraped. Bandage this over the eyes, and let it remain until morning. Then wash the eyes with a weak solution of an antiseptic. This will clarify the eyes."

Some ladies who have researched the readings and tried many of the suggestions given, report that the Irish potato poultices, if applied to tired eyes for just half an hour before that 'special evening,' does wonders.

Another common eyelid problem, today as then, is the cyst; case 1424-4 asked what the "little place" on the eyelid was and was told "Cysts—from a breaking of cellular forces." The cure was simple: "massage with pure Castor Oil."

The wearing of glasses, although helpful to vision, is thought by some to be a hindrance to beauty. Although contact lenses were available during Cayce's lifetime, they were the scleral lenses—almost as large as eyebaths and used only when imperative, for example by professional entertainers. The micro lens as we know it today was not invented until 1948 by Kevin Tuohy, and did not become popular until a good ten years later.

In attempting to obviate the wearing of glasses, 3549-1 asked how to improve vision. She was told that "When we remove the pressures of the toxic forces we will improve the vision." Then followed a practice which was given over and over for many reasons. "Also the head and neck exercise will be most helpful.

Take this regularly, not taking sometimes and leaving off sometimes, but each morning and each evening take this exercise regularly for six months and we will see a great difference. Sitting erect, bend the head forward three times, to the back three times, to the right side three times, to the left side three times, and then circle the head each way three times. Don't hurry through with it, but TAKE THE TIME to do it. We will get results."

When 2072-13 asked if she needed glasses, he told her "Not long off, but take the head and neck exercises and you can delay it some years yet."

An electrically driven vibrator was included in 303-2's instructions for gaining better vision. "The applications of the vibrations, especially in the first cervical or at the base of the brain and over the head . . . will stimulate for a better vision. Practice the circular motions for the head and neck, closing eyes AND SEEING SELF SEEING BETTER. This will create that reaction which brings practice to the nerve and muscular forces to that portion of the sensory system which has been disturbed."

Here visualization of the end result was added to the simple, but effective exercise.

Case 2533-6's question as to how to "eliminate the necessity of reading glasses" brought instructions for this exercise with a new twist. "By the head and neck exercises in the open. As ye walk for twenty to thirty minutes each morning. Now do not undertake it one morning and then say 'It rained and I couldn't get out' or 'I've got to go somewhere else' and think there aren't those despot conditions that rebel at not having their morning walk!"

The forces in a body are interwoven. One helps the other, or hinders as the case may be. A mother, 3925-1, asked if the treatments which Cayce prescribed for her daughter would improve her eyesight or would she need glasses?

"This is to strengthen the whole system, and with the forces in the system, is not necessary for this body to have glasses as yet, see?"

The causes of eye distress seem to be varied. Case 531-6,

troubled with a glare, was told that: "Such effects are from pressures that are hindrances, especially through the lymph circulation, through the soft tissues of the face, head and neck, by congestion and accumulation of poisons."

One of the aids to clear and brighten irritated eyes was: "Bathe these with a weak Glyco-Thymoline solution. Use an eye cup, and two parts of distilled water, preferably, to one part of the Glyco-Thymoline. This irritation is a part of the kidney disturbance that has come from the upsetting of the digestive forces." (3050-2)

Puffiness and discoloration around the eyes is a common problem; case 1158-38 had "puffs of yellow skin around eyes" and was told that this was caused by ". . . poor circulation, and the stimulation taken osteopathically once a week for three weeks and then leave off two or three weeks and then again these general relaxing treatments, will be most helpful."

Case 5021-1's left eye tired quickly, and had a lot of dark discoloration under it. Her problem was ". . . pressure upon the central nervous system. As these are gradually causing greater and greater distress, more and more pressure is put upon the kidneys. Thus the effects are as reflexes from the disturbances in the kidney area."

Case 257-254 asked "What makes eyes so heavy at times?" and was given a short and sweet answer: "Poor eliminations. Poison and toxic forces through the body."

Cayce gave one woman the basic cause of her dark circles under the eyes. He answered her question "Does the body eliminate properly" with a plain "NO" and then went on to add: ". . . the unequalized circulation, the effects of the digestion and of toxins in the system, cause the unequal distribution of the high hepatic circulation, causes poor eliminations. There are times when this is very good. This is especially shown in the system by the complexion and the texture as it were, in capillary eliminations, causing at times the circles under the eyes . . ." (1713-7)

Once again, the diet plays an enormous part and when asked

about specific diet hints for eyes, Cayce said: "If gelatin will be taken with raw foods, rather often that is, prepare raw vegetables such as carrots often with same, but do not lose the juice from the carrots; [grate them and eat them raw], we will help the vision." (5148-1)

"(Eat) that which is a well-balanced diet. But often use the raw vegetables which are prepared with gelatin. Use these at least three times each week. Those which grow above the ground, rather than those which grow below the ground. Do include, when these are prepared, carrots—with that portion, especially close to the top. It, [that is, this part of the carrot] may appear the harder and the less desirable, but it carries the vital energies, stimulating the optic reactions between kidneys and the optics or eyes." (3051-6)

The gift of sight is a very precious gift. Let those who have it treasure it, work to keep it and, whenever possible, improve it. If we agree that the soul does shine through the eyes, let its radiance pour through with joy and love unobstructed.

Teeth

To think that a smile could change the whole course of the world is truly something to ponder: "It is by thy smile and not a word spoken that the day may be made brighter for many a soul and in making the day brighter, even for a moment, ye have contributed to the whole world of affairs." (2794-3)

Just anyone can stand on a street corner and smile an infectious smile, and thereby contribute to the whole world of affairs.

What are the ingredients then, to keep our smiles shining brightly? Case 1467-8 was told that "There is no better dentifrice than soda and salt."

This mixture, equal portions of baking soda and table salt, was recommended time and again as a cleanser for teeth. If it was not advised for daily use, it was certainly suggested that it be used three to four times a week.

When 3484-1 asked "What is the best procedure for care of teeth?" she was told: "Have local attention and then take care of the teeth. Use equal combination of salt and soda for teeth and for massaging the gums. Don't use a brush [for massaging]; use your finger."

Case 457–11 asked what causes the gray film on teeth. All of us, at some time or another get a film on our teeth, even though it is not always gray. She was told: "The chemical balance in the system and the throw-off or discharge from the breath in the lungs. This [the breath] is a source from which the drosses are relieved from the system and thus passing through the teeth produce [evidences of] same on the teeth."

Here we have a perfect example of the eliminations through the respiratory system and evidence of poisons being released from the body. How to cope with these released poisons? Cayce suggested that "Keeping such [teeth] cleansed with an equal combination of Soda and Salt at least three to four times a week will cleanse these of this disturbance." He concluded with ". . . and use any good dentifrice once or twice a day."

In a reading for 2461–1 he was asked why lime forms on teeth, and for this particular person, in unusual thickness. The answer was in keeping with the previous reading quoted: "It is from the impurities—or toxic conditions through the system."

Tooth decay is a subject of interest to everyone, judging from the commercials on television. It was no different in 1943 when 2981–2 asked how to care for teeth so that there would be less decaying, and was told: "Use as a massage for the gums and teeth an equal combination of common Table Salt and Baking Soda" (our old friend) but was given a new trick to add: ". . . about once a month add one drop only of chlorine to a pint of water and rinse the mouth with this. DO NOT swallow it, but rinse the mouth and then brush the teeth." He explained that "This will preserve them, even aid in filling cavities."

"What can I do to keep my teeth for life" asked 3436–P–1? "You won't," she was told, "for these already need local attention. If there is kept the proper balance in the vitamins, it will help. But these precautions should begin—well, during the period of gestation is when they *should* begin—but a body should begin in at least the first or second year. The general care of teeth with a good dentifrice as well as with good massage for the gums will aid."

It seems, then, that care of the teeth should start in the womb. Most of us are a little late if we can read these words. But when Cayce was asked about preventing mottling of enamel and decay in children's teeth, he said that this can be done "By keeping a proper balance in the diet and in the protection from the ordinary causes—which are the lack of cleanliness." (3211-1)

Cayce formulated a solution which was recommended for treatment and prevention of gum disorders whenever the subject arose. The basic formula suggested started with "rain or snow water," but, in a later reading, proportions were changed for use with sea water. Basically the formula consists of prickly ash bark added to the water, which is then reduced to half by simmering. To this is added iodized salt, Atomidine, oil of peppermint and calcium chloride.

Dentists say that we could keep our teeth much longer if only our gums would remain healthy. Often the culprit for teeth having to be extracted *is* the gums, although "Where there is indicated that pus sacs are a portion of the roots of the teeth, remove them—for they only become a storehouse for poisons." (325-54)

Care for the gums was outlined for 274-5, who asked how often the formula should be used. "Once or twice a week" was the answer. "Apply a small quantity; or dip the finger into the solution, after it is shaken together, and massage the gums; or apply a small quantity to a tuft of cotton and massage inside and outside the gums, upper and lower. Where specific conditions in the teeth disturb, apply a small quantity on the end of a toothpick, with a tuft of cotton around same, to be sure, and rub along the edge of the gums. This will be found most effective. It will destroy the influences known as Riggs' disease or pyorrhea effects."

Case 257-13 was told to "Use the formula to stop the bleeding from the gums . . . and to keep teeth from tartar."

Although this is now available made up commercially from

the formula which Edgar Cayce gave, here is a simple version of the pyorrhea treatment:

"To six ounces of distilled water, add two ounces of Prickly Ash Bark. Reduce by simmering (not boiling) to two ounces. Strain and add powdered common Table Salt until we have a very thin paste.

"Rinse or rub gums with this once every two days until this trouble in the mouth and gums has subsided." (4436-2)

Traveling through Morocco one cannot help noticing that one of the most common bodily beautifiers is to extract the eye teeth and replace them with gold teeth. This is in evidence whenever the natives smile. During the twenties and thirties (and even now in some areas), it was the fashion in parts of Europe to replace missing teeth with gold ones. Cayce was asked if gold in the mouth caused bitterness. He said that "It does; NO teeth should ever be filled with heavy metals such as gold." (325-55)

> Now gold in the bank is a wonderful thing,
> And a woman looks nice with a nice gold ring,
> But, honey, take a tip, and the tip ain't cold,
> Your mouth's no place to carry your gold!
>
> I'm a gold tooth woman with the gold tooth blues
> 'Cause a gold tooth makes a woman look old! *

Although we shall go into cycles in more detail in a future chapter, it would be well to introduce the subject here. "The body replenishes itself every seven years in toto. What is acting today may be tomorrow another cycle of another portion's activity . . ." (988-10)

Specifically for the teeth: "Cycles change for the teeth during the second year of each [seven year life] cycle. During that year take at least three to four series of Calcios doses, or its equivalent, to supply calcium, and it will aid not only teeth but all the activities of the thyroid gland." (3051-3)

---

* From *In the Winter of Cities: Poems by Tennessee Williams*, copyright © 1956 by Tennessee Williams. Reprinted by permission of New Directions Publishing Corporation.

The thyroid was the gland meant in 5313-4's reading when he spoke of gaining "better control of the gland's activity which formulate the circulation through teeth and structural portions of the body."

For the non mathematical, the years [ages] to which Cayce referred for the teeth-change year of the complete life-cycle are: 2, 9, 16, 23, 30, 37, 44, 51, 58, 65, 72 and 79, and if you still have teeth after this, you should be giving your secrets out instead of reading these.

Calcios is no longer manufactured, but another dietary source of calcium that Cayce often suggested is chicken bones, especially the neck. He also suggested eating fish bones (from canned fish, of course). More about this in the chapter on diet.

Fluorine, a most important aspect of tooth care, will conclude this section on teeth. Back in 1943, a reading was given specifically for research in dentistry. At the outset, Cayce asked if this information was to be put to individual use, for that would entail one approach, or for universal use, as that would be another approach. He was assured that it would be for the latter.

He was questioned in this way: "Regarding the universal approach: Is it true, as it is thought that the intake of certain forms and percentages of fluorine in drinking water causes mottled enamel of the teeth?" "This is true, to be sure; but this is also untrue unless there is considered the other properties with which such is associated in drinking water.

"If there are certain percents of fluorine with free limestone, we will find it beneficial. If there are certain percents with indications of magnesium, sulphur and the like, we will have one motley, another decaying at the gum.

". . . It depends upon the combination, more than it does upon the quantity of fluorine itself. But, to be sure, too much fluorine in the water would make not so much in the teeth as it would in other elements or activities which may be reflected in teeth; not as the cause of same but producing a disturbance that may contribute to the condition.

"But where there is iron or sulphur or magnesium, be careful." (3211–1)

Now that you are familiar with the mechanics of a smile, do not hesitate to conjure one up. But remember, you only get out of a smile what you put into it.

Hands and Nails

The hands are the part of the body which represent the tools of action. They are symbols of directive principle of activity. Woven through the fabric of the readings runs a golden cord: "For the accomplishment comes in any direction through the doing . . . the DOING!"

Hands are things of great beauty as any lover of the dance will attest. In fact, in Indian dance it is the hands that tell the tale. This is also true in many other parts of the world: Indonesia, Hawaii and the South Pacific islands.

Did you ever know someone who would be speechless if his or her hands were tied? Often more can be conveyed with a gesture of the hand than with a lengthy explanation. In fact, hand language is international. In Italy, a supplement to the dictionary is published for foreigners in which one picture is truly worth at least ten words in any language.

Hands tell stories, not only by the lines in the palm of the hand, but by the very shape of the hand and the way that it is held or carried, or the strength with which you shake another's hand. The shape of the nails and their color will tell a story to anyone who has made a study of these details.

Case 3393-1's nails told another kind of story to Edgar Cayce: "The body then became lacking in sufficient quantities of iodine or potash, or potassium in the body, so that the glands of the thyroid cause disturbance—and have begun to make changes for the superficial circulation as related to the skin, nails, as well as portions of the digestive system."

The following excerpts will speak for themselves:

Q. "What causes fingernails to split and break?"

A. "This is a lack of the glandular forces, especially in the thyroid, which will be materially aided by the addition of the

A and D vitamin forces as combined with the B complex, for the general tonic for the body." (667–14)

Q. "What causes condition of fingernails?"

A. "This is from a poor activity of the thyroid and is part of the overemotional nature of the body, as the general nervous tension. Better assimilation and especially of the foods indicated, should change these. Keep these is such shape—the fingernails—that there is not the pulling into the quick, as this will cause great disturbance, but over the ends of the nails massage a saturated solution of vinegar and salt; using only the pure apple cider vinegar, and preferably Iodized Salt." (2452–1)

Q. "What is the cause of ridges or marking on fingernails?"

A. "The glandular disturbance as related to the thyroid. But the stimulations or the 'boosters' for the general system, and better eliminations established, should be sufficient in the present." (1770–5)

Q. "What will strengthen the fingernails against peeling and breaking?"

A. "The orange juice, the stimulation to the glandular circulation, and especially the diets of the potato peels." * (1102–2)

Q. "Is the breaking of fingernails due to a physical lack, or is it a natural result from work done?"

A. "In this particular case, it is something of both. This indicates the lack of proper assimilations or adjustments through the thyroid, or the lack of sufficient iodine in the system."

Q. "How should the iodine be supplied?"

A. "IN THE FOODS." (457–9)

* Author's note: See Chapter 5 re potato peels.

Case 288–42 was told "For those irritations as appear in the cuticle, bathe same with a weakened solution of Atomidine." About a week later, she wrote to report that "After using Atomidine a few days the breaking-out cleared."

For hangnails, 308–1 was instructed, "Where hangnails have been produced on hands, we would use any antiseptic on small pieces of cotton . . . Small quantities as of Atomidine or of *any* antiseptic that is *healing*, though carries not a great deal of therapeutic value in its activity." This was for a child of eight years of age; the cure could not be too strong."

Q. "What can I do to keep my finger nails from splitting?"

A. "Add the vitamins necessary so that the glandular forces, and especially the thyroid are improved. [At this point, Cayce gave specific instructions for correcting the glandular imbalance, then continued.] Also massage the fingernails with Atomidine. It may stain for a bit at first, but get the system going well and we will find this will be different." (2448–1)

With the excerpt from the reading of 1467–7, a new aspect is brought in.

Q. "What should I do to keep fingernails from splitting?"

A. "This is a lack of proper amount of calcium in the system."

"A lack of calcium is indicated in the body, by the very color or nature of the toenails and fingernails—and even by the condition which exists at times in the hair on various portions of the body." (2518–1)

He recommended that calcium should be taken cyclically, five days at a time and then leave off a few days, then taking again.

Q. "What causes deep ridges in thumbnail and what treatments?"

A. "These are the results of the activities of the glandular forces and the addition of those foods which carry the large quantities of calcium will make bettered conditions. Take often chicken neck, chew it, cook this well, the feet and those portions of the fowl, and we will find it will add calcium to the body. Also eat bones of fish, such as canned fish; also parsnips and oyster plant—all of these, of course in their regular season. Wild game of any kind, but chew the bones of same." (5192-1)

A sure deterrent to beautiful hands, and one of our own making, is the habit of biting the nails. Cayce had a great deal to say on habits. As a definition he gave "The subconscious mind is both consciousness and thought or spirit-consciousness. Hence may be best classified, in the physical sense, as a habit." (262-10)

And he told 553-1: "For thou hast seen that the purpose and the will make for desires that grow—as do habits that may infest even the mind as habits do the body and its attributes."

Specifically about nail-biting, 475-1 was given: "This is the effect of nervousness—from the gnawing that has been indicated that has been existent for some time in the system, see? and with these corrections and with the tendency for the body to watch or be careful with self this may be eliminated from the habits of the body. For, if we take away the cause, the habit is more easily changed. *For, we correct habits by forming others*—that's everybody."

Q. "What is the cause of nail biting and how can I prevent it?"

A. "This is produced especially by nervous reactions in system, and is a form of habit. With the removal of those tendencies that make for the inability of coordination of impulse and activity, and reducing these to normalcy, then the *will* in self to stop, change or alter such conditions becomes an easy, or easier matter." (268-2)

Q. "How can nervousness be controlled as far as biting finger-nails?"

A. "Make self conscious of its activities in the use of extremities, and make for the *voluntary* actions to *be* voluntary, and *not* as involuntary. Keep the hands busy at something else and it will keep them out of the mouth." (1739-7)

Q. "What can I do to cure the habit of biting and picking skin on fingers causing soreness and disfiguration?"

A. "Change your mind." (3583-1)

Man is capable of doing ANYTHING if he chooses—and puts some energy behind the choice. To break a habit, then, follow Cayce's advice. Change your mind, choose to do other than the habit. Replace the involuntary action which is the habit with something constructive. "For each soul, each mind, each entity is endowed with its choice. And the choice is the result of the application of self in relationships to that which is its ideal—and finds manifestation in what individuals call habit, or subconscious activity. Yet it has its inception in that of choice." (830-2)

Case 758-27 posed a very interesting question about her eight-year-old child. She wanted to know if the use of the right hand or the left should be developed.

"Right. While the body is tended to be in the nature of both-handed, or super dextrous, yet in the developing of the body—with the positions of the muscular forces and the position of the heart itself in the body—the *right* would be much better. Notice the positions when individuals are left-handed: it is more often the position of the heart!"

Case 1533-1 wanted to know the cause of her hands being hard and dry, "and at times to form little water blisters?" She was told: "The poor circulation, and the lack of the activities or coordination between the glandular system and the eliminations."

Case 2769-1 also had trouble with her palms; they and her feet were "burning." She wanted to know what could be done and the answer to which her question gave rise included a "treasure."

"After the first of the massages following the fume bath—these will disappear—that is after the first series, see?

"If there is the desire for that which will be almost a perfect skin lotion, use on same a compound prepared in this manner:

> 2 oz. Rose Water
> ½ oz. Usoline
> ½ tsp. Lanolin, dissolved

Rubbing this on the hands, in the palms and on the feet will heal, and prevent burning—or the roughness or those tendencies for rash."

This lotion, although it needs to be shaken each time it is used, contains ingredients which are inexpensive, and finding this formula was worth all the time spent researching the subject of hands. (Russian white oil or Nujol was often substituted for Usoline.)

Feet

Our feet are our direct material contact with the earth. It is said that the feet are a symbol of the soul since they support the body and keep man upright. You will remember that the washing of the feet was a very important ceremony enacted at the Last Supper. Christ washed the feet of the disciples, much to the embarrassment of Peter. "What I do thou knowest not now, but thou shalt know hereafter" said the Lord. (John 13:7)

What symbolic mystery lies in the feet? Jesus had his feet washed with oils and dried with the hair of Mary Magdalene. In Oriental art, the Buddha is depicted with flowers and other designs painted on the soles of his feet, representing the spiritual strides which man makes in a lifetime. Toward this end they deserve some extra consideration.

In 1917, the doctors Fitzgerald and Bowers wrote a book called

Zone Therapy* which dealt with the relief of ailments through pressure on the feet at various points which corresponded to the nerve linkages with the troubled area. This healing art is also known as Reflexology.

The subject of feet appeared in the readings often enough to be able to extract a pattern of treatments for various foot ailments. To include a section on feet in a book devoted to beauty may at first appear strange, but if you have ever been bothered by a corn, callous or ingrown toenail, and tried to radiate beauty through the pain, you will understand its inclusion.

Case 602-3 asked Cayce to describe the derangement of her right foot. After obliging her with the requested information, he offered as an epilogue: "For, as may be seen, there's nearly a third of the bones of a body in the feet! These make for then, the necessity of these being kept in accord."

When 69-5 asked for an explanation of her foot trouble, she was told: "This is part of the effect from those pressures, which will be materially aided if there is proper massage given with the oils along the limbs and feet.

"For, as has been indicated, when the circulation is slowed, the extremities are the areas that obtain the least of the proper impulse for the removal of used energies. Thus we find, this condition will be materially aided by the massage."

Case 1770-5 asked: "What causes excessive dryness or peeling of skin on bottom of feet?" She was told: "Poor circulation. Hence the needs for the massage and oil rubs, which should include the limbs—of course—and especially the feet, with adjustments in the muscular forces and bursa of the feet." (Peanut oil and olive oil in equal parts was suggested for the oil rubs.)

Another specific for faulty circulation was given for 3776-9. "It would be well if the feet and the limbs were bathed in very warm water to increase circulation in this portion of the system. Put mustard in the water when this is done." There are two kinds of mustard in general use, black and white. The white is

* William H. Fitzgerald and Edwin F. Bowers, *Zone Therapy* (Columbus. Ohio: I. W. Long Publishing Co.).

a smaller plant and the milder of the two. The black mustard is the one which contains medicinal properties. It contains a good deal of sulphur, forms an ingredient of Indian curries and is said to prevent dyspepsia. The powder, mixed with very hot water, is used to soak the feet of those who have been caught in drenching rain, in order to prevent chills, as given in many old herbals.

The following excerpts mentioned poor circulation and will give you some idea as to the number of ailments to which this gives rise:

Q. "What causes the unusual perspirations of the feet?"

A. "This is caused by the circulation being disturbed, especially through the hepatics. This is produced by poisons and the attempt of the body to throw them off. When the portions are cut off in the lower portions of the body [from improper circulation] they accumulate there." (759-9)

Q. "What causes aching and burning of feet, especially in warm weather?"

A. "This is caused by poor circulation and acid in the system." (779-21)

Q. "There has appeared a crustiness between the toes; how can I help this?"

A. "The use of the exercise of rising on the toes—with only stockings or very light slippers on the feet—will make a great deal of difference in the general *circulation*.

"Local application of any solution with alcohol, or the pure grain alcohol, weakened, will remove the disturbance." (480-45)

Q. "What causes the toes to itch?"

A. "Improper circulation to the lower portions of the body . . . we may use very small quantities of sulphur in the shoes." (287-4)

Of all the many remedies, massage seems to be the hands-down winner for this problem. The three following excerpts should prove beneficial:

"This [excessive cracking in the bones of the feet] comes from a lack of proper circulation. A gentle but thorough massage of the limbs DOWNWARD, with Cocoa Butter, especially through the feet and bursa of the heel and the ball of the foot, and across the toes, will aid—this done once or twice a week." (1158-21)

"Also use the rubs with the compound indicated. Use all the skin will absorb: To four ounces Russian White Oil, or Nujol, add: Witch Hazel, two ounces; rubbing alcohol, two ounces; Oil of Sassafras, five minims; Tincture of Benzoin, one ounce. Shake the solution together before it is poured for massaging, for both the Sassafras and the tincture of Benzoin will tend to separate from the oils. This may be used to massage the whole body." (243-17)

"When 265-15 asked what would relieve the swelling in her feet and ankles she was told: "Rub the lumbar area with Olive Oil and Myrrh so that the circulation may be eased through these portions of the body. Where there are pressures from long sitting or from lack of activity, these cause a tendency for the blood to flow to the feet without the ability to flow away. Use equal parts of Olive Oil and Tincture of Myrrh. Heat the Oil to add the Myrrh, massaging this into the lumbar and sacral areas."

Detailed directions for the massage of limbs affecting the feet were given to 1968-7 when she asked: "What causes occasional pain in right ankle?" "Strain, and this from poor eliminations. But when the massage is given for the limbs, commence first at the hips and around either side of the limbs, massaging downwards. This should go with the sciatic center as well as around and under the knee, over the calf of the leg and down to the very feet themselves, massaging the soles of the feet. Then come backwards, you see; that is, from the feet back towards the body. After the second or third of such massages, this disturbance should be eliminated."

Problems of the feet often are manifestations of trouble in another area. The lumbar and sacral regions were mentioned in direct relationship to the feet when 5609-1 asked if he should continue wearing his arch supporters. Cayce answered him with: "Why not make the corrections and do without the arch supporters? They will be all right as long as the condition exists, but they will gradually grow worse unless we make the corrections [osteopathically] in the lumbar and sacral regions."

When 325-7 asked about relieving the pain in the feet, she was told that "This is produced from the poor ELIMINATIONS through the system AND the impaired circulation . . ." He recommended that she occasionally bathe the feet in a saturated solution of Sal-Soda as hot as the body could stand when the feet were soaked in it.

Q. "What causes the cramp in the big toe?"

A. "The association and the connection as it were with the glandular system. Relief may be obtained not only by emptying, but cleansing and purifying the colon, and by a massage to the centers from which the impulses are received to the lower portion of the foot." (337-24)

Q. "What causes the breaking out and itching on the feet and how can it be cured?"

A. "This is from poor eliminations. Local applications may be made of Witch Hazel when ready for retiring." (781-2)

Another reference is made to Witch Hazel in a reading for 903-16, who asked what would stop the condition that occurred between her toes and was told to "Use occasionally Witch Hazel full strength to reduce this itching. Bathe the feet . . . and bathe them often, in salt water."

So much for the inner workings of the body affecting the feet. Here, now, are some treasures from the readings which will help anybody who is troubled with corns, callouses or ingrowing toenails:

As for ingrown toenails: "and for the condition of the toes and nails, use Baking Soda moistened with Castor Oil. Put this under the points or edges where ingrown toenails give disturbance. This may make it sore for one time, but rub it off with Spirits of Camphor. These may make for roughening but it will rid the body of those disturbances of ingrown toenails." (5104-1)

This formula has been tried and found successful by many. Should it, however, fail to work, here is an alternative treatment. "Once each week we would use the Atomidine as a massage for the soles of the feet and as a dressing for the toenails. This will change the disturbance with ingrowing nails. Lift up the nail and put small parts of cotton saturated with Atomidine under edge of the toenail. Use this at least once each week." (2988-1)

Case 2455-3 had a thick nail and a growth under her big toe and wanted to know what to do about it. Cayce told her "For the conditions in the lower limbs and the feet we would massage these thoroughly with Peanut Oil.

"For the conditions of hardening, as on toe, we would use a mixture of Baking Soda and Castor Oil. Do not bind up, but massage this on after the feet *and* lower limbs—from the knees downward—have been thoroughly massaged with the Peanut Oil. Do this at least three to four times a week; and the conditions— it will be found—will disappear."

Case 276-4 wanted to know what caused the growth on her foot and what should be used if it recurred. This question gave rise to one of those wonderful answers which pertained to anyone:

"This was caused from irritation. Massaging with Baking Soda which has been dampened with Spirits of Camphor will be good for ANYONE having callous places or any attendant growths on feet; for it will remove them entirely."

The same advice was given for 1309-7, who was troubled with corns. She asked for the cause and treatment of same, and was told that "Misfitting of shoes is usually the cause of corns. The best treatment is to use Camphor and Soda. Wet plain Baking Soda with Spirits of Camphor and apply nightly until corn is removed." Then he added as a word of warning for the future, "Then fit the shoes nominally."

Speaking from personal experience, this does not happen over-night. It might take as long as two months, but as Cayce often said, these disturbances do not come in a day, why expect them to leave in a day?

"What will cure bunions?" asked 983–1. "Massage each evening . . . before retiring, with Soda [plain baking] damped with Spirits of Camphor, on the bunions themselves." Cayce then added, unsolicited, "As to the hardened places on the soles of the feet, or just between the toes or points of the toes, massage these thoroughly with equal parts of Olive Oil and Tincture Of Myrrh—and these will soften considerably."

Case 1140–1 asked if she should have the large joint or bunion operated upon. "With these drainages, these conditions should be materially aided. And massage same rather, morning and evening, with equal portions of Olive Oil and Tincture of Myrrh. With the drainages, with the manipulative forces, with the organs balanced, these should disappear without operative forces."

Apparently 1140–1 needed other attention *with* the local application, as did 365–2. She told of one bunion already existing and another one starting and wanted to know if it would be necessary to wear a special mechanical device, or would treatments correct the condition? "Treatments will correct the condition, to be sure, preferably. To wear the specially prepared shoe would be well, even while treatment are being given.

"The treatments would be proper manipulation of the bursas in the feet and ankles osteopathically; and one day massage the bunions or those portions of the pedals that disturb with pure Castor Oil. The next day dampen plain Baking Soda with sufficient Spirits of Camphor to wet same and massage this into the places that tend to be sore or callous. Keep up the treatment and this will disappear."

There were other formulas recommended for callouses which are included for reference. "Massage it [callous] with a preparation made in this manner:

"To one half ounce melted Mutton Tallow [one-half ounce in weight], while still warm and in solution, add:

20 minims. Oil of Turpentine
40 minims. Spirits of Camphor

"Use this to massage the bottoms of the feet each evening."
(307-6) "In reference to the feet and the callous places—we would
massage these places night and morning with a mixture of a
tablespoonful of Castor Oil and a quarter teaspoonful of Baking
Soda. Mix these ingredients thoroughly together and massage. Of
course, this whole quantity would not be used all at once, unless
necessary. After the massaging is completed, if necessary sponge
off any excess in those areas. This will bring better forces for this
body." (2334-1) "Where there are irritations in portions of the
feet, or in the ball of the foot, we would massage same with an
equal combination of Olive Oil and Tincture of Myrrh each evening when ready to retire. Heat the oil to add the myrrh. Massage
this thoroughly into the soles of the feet and *especially* in that
area where there is the callous condition. Of morning before
putting on the hose, do the same thing; rest only a few minutes
after rubbing same into the body and then put on the hose, see?"
(1771-3)

One reading might be of interest to readers living in a very
cold climate. A young girl (sixteen), 276-7, wanted to know the
correct treatment for frostbite, and was told: "The better as we
find, is petrol—or coal oil—massaged, and taken in VERY
SMALL quantities." "Taken internally?" she asked incredu-
lously. "Taken internally and rubbed on too!" she was told in
no uncertain manner.*

Many readings advised that the feet should be kept dry.
"Those tendencies for congestion and cold in the bronchi and
throat . . . Keep the feet dry, keep out of the night air. Keep
the general care of the system, that the body is kept warm—
especially the feet . . ." (288-32) "Be mindful that the feet are
kept dry; that there is not too much draft." (304-25) "Conditions
in the present are rather acute . . . cold, congestion . . . toxic

---

* Author's note: What might constitute a "VERY SMALL" QUANTITY?
One drop a day?

strep. . . . Do not be negligent about the care of the body in keeping the feet warm and dry especially." (667-6)

". . . Let the body remain quiet. KEEP THE FEET WARM. Massage and make for the general rest." A sedative was also recommended. (6010-14)

Considering that Cayce advised walking as one of the best exercises, (see Chapter 7) it would be a good idea to perfect the feet toward that phase of endeavor.

SUMMARY

I. Eyes

A. Ascertain that the cervical and upper dorsal vertebrae are manipulated and aligned.
B. For irritated lids: Poultices of scraped, old Irish potatoes.
C. For cysts on lids: Massage with castor oil.
D. To improve vision: Head and neck exercises as outlined.
E. To brighten irritated eyes: Bathe with solution of one-third Glyco-Thymoline to two-thirds distilled water in an eye cup.
F. Diet to aid eyes: Raw grated carrots in a mold of gelatin.

II. Teeth

A. Dentifrice: Equal parts of table salt and baking soda, at least three or four times a week.
B. To help prevent cavities: Once a month rinse mouth before brushing teeth with a pint of water to which one drop of chlorine has been added. DO NOT SWALLOW.
C. Take series of calcium during the second year of each seven year cycle.
D. Do not fill teeth with gold.

III. Hands and Nails

  A. For strengthening nails: Apply pure apple cider vinegar and iodized table salt mixed to a paste.
  B. For problem cuticles: Massage with a weakened solution of Atomidine.
  C. Skin lotion for hands:

  2 oz. Rose water
  ½ oz. Usoline (or Nujol)
  ½ tsp. Lanolin (dissolved)

IV. Feet

  A. Watch eliminations and circulation.
  B. Massages: Various formulas, perhaps the easiest is equal parts of olive and peanut oil.
  C. Corns: Apply baking soda moistened with spirits of camphor twice a day until they disappear.
  D. Callouses: Massage with olive oil and tincture of myrrh, equal parts.

  To remove callouses under the foot: Massage with baking soda moistened with spirits of camphor.
  E. Ingrown toenails: Mixture of baking soda and castor oil put under corners of nail and wiped off with spirits of camphor. Or place cotton soaked in Atomidine beneath corners of ingrowing nails.

CHAPTER *5* *Glorifying the Crowning Glory*

GUIDE TO HAIR CARE

DESCRIBE SOME man or woman you know to another person. You will most probably start with the color or length of the hair. Hair has figured in literature, history and legend to a great degree. In the Bible, Samson's downfall was brought about by the haircut which Delila gave him; Lady Godiva's long blonde tresses were all that shielded her nudity from the gaze of the defiant townsman; Rapunzel was beseeched to let down her hair; Melisande does let her hair down in Debussy's opera, *Pelleas and Melisande,* and the hero spends one full scene caressing the long blonde locks which cascade from the turret window (to music, to be sure).

Hair figures in all manner of symbology. When it is shaved from the crown of the head—as the monks do—it is a symbol of contrition for the shortcomings of the lower nature. Gaskell, however, in his *Dictionary of the Sacred Language of All Scriptures and Myths,* gives hair as representing the highest qualities of the lower nature, a symbol of faith, intuition of truth.*

* George Arthur Gaskell, *Dictionary of Sacred Language of All Scriptures and Myths* (London: G. Allen & Unwin Ltd., 1923).

One thing is sure; according to the Bible, every hair on our head is numbered. (Luke 12:7)

Asked how often the hair should be washed, Cayce answered simply "When it's needed." (275-31) Nothing could be simpler.

Poor hair condition or loss

Case 365-2's hair was "falling out very much" and she was understandably concerned. She asked "Will this condition stop as my body improves, or can I do something to prevent this?" She was told that "This will naturally improve as the body builds, and as the proper balance is made in the blood supply of this body . . . these conditions will improve. For the specific conditions of the scalp however, we would suggest the following:

"When hair is washed, treat it with Olive Oil and an equal portion of Pure Castile (that is liquid, see?); then massage the scalp with a little pure grain alcohol—or 20 percent solution of pure grain alcohol.

"This will not only invigorate the scalp, but will make a tendency for the growth of the hair."

The most frequently suggested treatment for the hair is a massage with crude oil. Not something to be rushed, but a massage that should last about half an hour. It was also recommended that the massage be given with an electrically driven vibrator, using the suction cup attachment.

Case 275–42, a twenty-one-year-old, asked for the best treatment for her hair. "Occasionally" said Cayce, "there should be used the crude oil first, then the shampoo, that is of the Olive Oil base—that will make for, with the egg, a cleansing for the body."

To 480–23 he explained the cause of "the falling out of the hair." "This is caused by a lack of activity through the glands that are secreting from the system the elements necessary for the portions of the thyroids which affect the circulation to the scalp."

She was told that "The diet affects this principally, although the scalp would be stimulated by a massage, which may be had with *properties that aid the scalp circulation.*" Now comes the answer to the crude oil's action: "Rub a small quantity of crude oil into the scalp once or twice a month and this would be sufficient *to renew the cells that produce hair.*" There was a proviso however, depending upon the gastric flow in the digestive forces and the general circulation of the body.

One reading concerning hair loss rather stuns the imagination. Case 4086-1 was told: "For these [disturbances] are rather the activities in the sensory and sympathetic nervous system, and arise from the body attempting to improve in a selfish manner upon what nature had intended for the body to be."

She then asked if "childbirth caused this condition." He answered, "It only aggravated—it is not the source of the condition but too much drying out of the scalp . . . to improve upon nature. BE NATURAL—YOU'LL BE MUCH MORE ATTRACTIVE."

Here then, is a case of someone with selfish motives, trying to improve upon nature and nature backfiring in the form of hair loss. Case 5609-1, one of whose problems was hair loss, asked whether the trouble was localized or throughout certain areas. The answer received, if read carefully, could shed some light on the way many of our problems are treated today. Cayce said: "We have given the condition as exists! Localized to be sure, if we consider that as being the trouble. The *trouble*—this is the effect—the effects are being treated, *not* the cause!"

This is like so many modern attitudes. When there is pain, one takes a pain killer for relief, rather than trying to discover the *cause* of the pain. A symptom is just a warning that attention is required somewhere.

"What kind of shampoo is best for my hair?" asked a twenty-year-old (1532-3). *"Plain soap and water* is best for ANY hair" was the surprising answer. He went on: "Any stimulant that carries a small quantity of Bay Rum is very good."

The statement "plain soap and water" might seem to contradict the previous excerpt advising Castile soap, but it must be remembered that Cayce treated each individual at his or her own level for specific needs. It might be conjectured that this twenty-year-old had put her faith in some very expensive shampoo, and because of its high price used it too sparingly or infrequently for a sufficient cleansing of the hair and scalp. Cayce's objective here might have been to emphasize the cleansing rather than the medium. He might have meant "plain soap" whether it had a vegetable oil base (Castile) or animal fat base (regular) as opposed to fancy or highly perfumed detergent-type shampoos.

This demonstrates perfectly how important it is to realize that Cayce's readings were given for specific individuals. If we are to benefit from the readings, it must not be in the use of a specific treatment given for an individual, but to use this information to gain a deeper understanding of the subject in question.

Dry scalp was a problem which appeared often and the treatment given for this was a small amount of white Vaseline* rubbed into the scalp. Case 633–12's "dryness on scalp" was attributed to poor circulation and nervousness. The suggestion was to "have a thorough massage or shampoo with pure Tar Soap—at least once a week—and then to massage a little White Vaseline into the scalp after such a shampoo."

Case 276–10 was troubled with oily hair and wanted to know the cause and "what can be done to decrease the oils?" "The condition arises from . . . the poor coordination between the superficial and deeper circulation by poisons in the system." He suggested that she "use a cleanser of crude oil for the scalp," then to "clear same with grain alcohol—NOT WOOD OR DE-NATURED, but GRAIN alcohol—solution ten or twenty to one; one ounce of the grain alcohol to twenty ounces of water, this to cleanse same afterwards. This, as we find, will make for the natural tones for the hair."

For specific cases of dandruff, 2336–1 was given: "Use Listerine at one shampoo and Lavoris at the next. These will eliminate dandruff." Other readings which recommend this treatment suggest that it be applied after the shampoo. Of the two prepa-

---

* Author's note: Use sparingly.

rations used, one is acid reacting, the other alkaline. This interchanging of the two properties was suggested for a number of problems, among them as an aid to stop smoking and as a treatment for gum infections. (Although the preparations differed, the interchanging properties—acid and alkaline—were employed.)

Case 257 seemed to have a lot of trouble with her hair. In her twelfth reading from Cayce she was told in response to her question of why there was so much dandruff, that if she were to "Use Listerine . . . there won't be so much." She then asked what caused the scalp to itch and was told: "It is caused by irritation, which is produced by the accumulations in the system. The digestion is bad, and the nerves are kept on edge. Use the Listerine twice a week on the hair."

In her two hundred and tenth reading, she was still having trouble with her hair and was told: "Keep the head washed, cleansed with a pure mild soap; using after same Listerine or ANY of a mild use of alcohol. BUT WASH THE HAIR AND SCALP OFTEN."

"Will you give a prescription for a solution that will make straight hair wave, if possible without heat?" asked a sixteen-year-old back in the days when curling tongs were the only way to give straight hair a curl. She was told that "if the pits of the lowly persimmon—with the bark of the roots of the tree—are distilled, adding only the preservatives as necessary for the keeping of same, and used as a massage for a period into the scalp of individuals, it will make the hair wave—even kinky if so desired." (276-7)

Should anyone like to try it, please let us know the results.

Superfluous hair

In the search for the fine balance which we consider perfection, we are often troubled with too much or too little. Not infrequently, bald men have luxurious beards or body hair. Short of circus performers, few women will welcome hair other than on the head, despite the fact that it is a natural part of our epidermis. The readings, in nearly all cases, attributed the cause of superfluous hair to a glandular imbalance: "A glandular condition, as combined with a disturbance in the general circulation. Do not disturb, or use any special application other than the reaction in the glandular forces to the thyroids to make better activity there; and this done more in manipulation [osteopathically] than by drugs." (2153–5)

"Superfluous hair or moles are the activities of the glands, especially of the thyroids, being over-effective or overactive in the system. To correct the system so that a balance is kept will make for a better tendency to equilibrium." (263–1) "This, again, is from an inactivity and the allowing of overactivity in certain portions of the thyroid gland. For, this is the portion in its balance that keep the body forces in balance, adding to or taking from the system that to aid in the growth of hair or nails and in keeping an equilibrium. So, with the corrections of these conditions, and there being then better indications and the correct flow of this glandular secretion, these should gradually disappear. For these conditions use only such things as to correct the system, not any mechanical or chemical forces to remove these, see?" [When she asked if the electric needle should be used, she received an emphatic] "No, indeed." (2582–1) "This is from the glandular disturbance to an excessive activity in the thyroid. Thus the needs of this purifying, this cleansing . . . and also the care of the circulation in the skin itself. This will disappear when the circulation is set normally." (2680–1)

When 1947–4 asked for a formula for destroying superfluous hair which would not injure the skin in any way, "There's no such animal!" he said, but added "This may best be done by diet AND the applications to the skin for keeping the pores open *and* the body actions better [eliminations]."

Case 3081–3 was told that "This is just a part of the body's own consciousness that it is meeting, or karmic conditions." (See Chapter 10.)

And 3341–1 was given quite a sermon in response to her question. "Better be glad you've got it, than to have other things that

would cause a great deal more trouble by trying to remove same!"
His advice to her was: "But if ye pray right, live right, ask for it
to be removed, ye may wash it off with lye soap."

How many problems might be solved by leading an ethical
life? Which had the power here, the correct living accompanied
by prayer, or the lye soap?

Color

In an age in which changing one's hair color is almost as easy
as changing one's hair style, Cayce's suggestions might seem a
little old-fashioned. But, in his day, hair color suggestions were
for the natural coloring of the hair, the giving to the body the
necessary forces to prevent hair graying, and to restore the natural
color after graying had started. His explanations are certainly
worthy of study in order to gain a deeper understanding of our
bodies' functionings.

Case 3051–3 asked if "tablets that I take restore color to
hair?" "No! if the juice of potato peelings is taken regularly
(two or three times a week) it will keep the hair nearer to its
normal color than all other forms of chemical preparations."

Potato peelings, even more specifically, peelings of Irish potatoes, were mentioned many times in connection with activity
for improving the condition of hair.

Q. "How can I keep my hair from turning gray?"

A. "The citrus fruit juices and the regular weekly use of the
juice from the Irish potato peel. Peel the potatoes and make a
soup of the peelings, see? Take this weekly." (2011–2)

One "gourmet" staff member of ARE makes a weekly pot of
potato peel soup which she creams and whips up in her blender,
topping it with a parsley sprig before serving. It is considered
quite a treat to be invited for dinner the night she prepares her
'hair conditioning meal.'

Case 2582–44 was interested in knowing if a popular hair color restorative of the period would prevent her hair from turning gray. She was given a quick "NO!" Then Cayce continued: "This will not prevent hair from turning gray. Rather we would use the massage in the hair of a small quantity of crude oil, followed by a good shampoo, and occasionally the massaging of a small quantity of pure hog lard into the scalp and leaving it overnight —just before the shampoo. This will not make the hair too oily, but will make for better conditions."

Sounds rather unappetizing, doesn't it? A more detailed explanation for the inner condition was given 3904-1, for whom he also advised the use of pure hog lard to be left on overnight. To her he explained: "As we find, there are conditions causing disturbances with this body. These are because of improper coordination of the activities of the inner and outer glandular forces as related to the thyroid. This allows for deficiencies in certain chemical forces, especially as related to the epidermis, or the activities in the toes and the fingers and the hair. These are distressing to the whole body."

A beautiful insight into hair color was revealed to 275-31, who wanted to know "how to keep blonde hair blonde." She was told that: "If the developments of a body are natural conditions, that this should grow to be a different color—by the forces in the system that make for pigments that change color, it is going against natural conditions to attempt to change or alter same! But" [he added compassionately to the darkening blonde twenty-year-old], "if the products whose basic forces are tar or pine elements are used for the cleansing, bicarbonate of soda in the rinsing water will make for those influences that will keep nearer to uniformity in the shading of hair. Heaping teaspoonful (bicarbonate of soda) to two gallons of water, the rinsing water to be sure. But . . . it must be thoroughly worked into the scalp and roots of hair, as well as the outer portion or it'll streak."

Case 1431-2's hair was turning dark at the roots, and she was only eighteen. At this age, such things are magnified out of all proportion. But Cayce told her to just "Use an Olive Oil shampoo. This as we find would be the better way." But, she was told,

"Shampoo it at least once each week."

When 982-5 asked what would restore her natural color to hair and make it more manageable, she was told: "If the scalp were massaged at least once every week with the Crude Oil and then cleansed with a weak solution of grain alcohol, and then followed by the White Vaseline rub, this will restore color, will thicken hair and make it more brilliant in its lustre."

What a promise! She surely started massaging the minute she got home.

The conditioning of one's hair today is even more important than in Cayce's time. The ease with which today's woman can abuse her hair is greater than the many so called 'conditioners' which are available in every drug store, supermarket and department store. A visit to a beauty salon is for today's woman as commonplace as going to a movie. While there, her hair may be rolled on rollers, twisted into metal clips and then dried artificially with hot air. The hair and scalp may be exposed to a variety of chemicals which change its texture, color or the way in which it grows. In the dressing, the hair may be teased, sprayed with more chemicals to stiffen it, pinned, intertwined with or suffocated by artificial hair made from any one of a number of synthetic fibers. Once arranged in this manner, it is sometimes allowed to remain for days without brushing or massaging the scalp. Some of today's hair styles appear as though they would prefer to be dusted with a feather duster than be brushed. However, fashion seems to be directing itself toward a more natural feeling. The beauty of the hair, condition and line is again becoming more important than the display of the stylists' virtuosity.

Thus ends the first part of our homage to beauty, the part which deals with the outer person. Of the divisions of the human body, Cayce gave: "Know that there is the influence of body, of mind, of soul. These are manifested in the material plane as an individual entity. Just as the Father, the Son, the Holy Spirit is an individual entity. Just as time and space and patience are the individual manifestation of that Spirit-Body in the experience of man."

As we are in a physical world, the first two parts of this book have been devoted to the body; the second part will deal with the inner workings. The third attempts to deal with a variety of influences and mind's and spirit's action upon the body. So, read on. Don't be a third of a person, for: "So seldom is it considered by all, that spirituality, mentality and the physical being are all one; yet may indeed separate and function one without the other—and *at the expense of the other*. Make them cooperate, make them one in their purpose." (307-10)

SUMMARY

I. Poor hair condition or loss

    A. For falling hair, use potato peelings (cooked or in soup) in diet.

    B. Massage head with crude oil one half hour with electric vibrator, rinse with ten to twenty percent solution of pure grain alcohol, shampoo with olive oil or Castile shampoo.

    C. For dandruff, clean hair meticulously; apply Listerine to scalp.

II. Superfluous hair

    A. This is usually a glandular condition.

    B. Attempt to solve problem mechanically (through osteopathy or chiropractic adjustments) and by diet rather than external chemical applications.

III. Color

To help prevent graying, use juice of potato peelings three times a week.

Part II

THE   INNER

CHAPTER *6*   *Food for the Body*

INSIGHTS INTO NUTRITION
AND SPECIAL DIETS

IT SEEMS that weekly someone is discovering some new slant on diet: how to get thin on gin and grapefruit juice; how to reduce incidence of heart disease with safflower oil; how to balance your Yin and Yang by eating brown rice three times a day. A good word can be said about many of these diets that are currently popular, for they do have something that is valid: an initiation into self-discipline and a breaking out of old ruts. Most of these have dealt with the correction of one fault or another, too many of which are blatantly obvious in the American diet.

Malnutrition in the affluent society is almost as prevalent as undernourishment in the ghetto.

It has been said before, but it is worth repeating here—and not for laughs: "America, you are digging your grave with your knife and fork." We should remember that the purpose of eating is *to nourish the human body*, not to cater to its appetites, since it is true that you are what you eat. Going one step further, the Cayce wisdom concluded: "We are, physically and mentally, what we eat and what we think." (288–38)

In this garden of earthly delights it is the apples we are told NOT to eat that seem to whet our appetites. But consider for a moment that old serpent 'habit' that builds those appetites. The apples in this twentieth century Eden are likely to be chocolate candy bars, rich pastries and soda pop, a fact that hardly needs statistical confirmation. Just look at your grocery list. The explanations which follow are food for both mind and body.

A most neglected practice is the daily intake of pure water—the source of life, the glue that holds our dietary structure together. In the Indian Vedas—holy scriptures—water is referred to as Mâtritamâh, or the superlative of 'maternal'. And like the proverbial Jewish mother, water is too often taken for granted. Let us give it the attention it deserves.

Cayce advised to "Always drink plenty of water, before meals and after meals." He explained that "when any food value enters the stomach, it immediately becomes a storehouse or a medicine chest that may create all the elements necessary for proper digestion within the system. If this first is acted upon by pure water, the reactions are more nearly normal." Then follows what could become a lifelong good habit: "Also, therefore, each morning upon arising, first take a half to three-quarters of a glass of warm water . . . not so hot that it is objectionable, not so tepid that it makes for sickening. But this will clarify the system of poisons." (311–4)

For those of you who are still wondering how bad eliminations can create skin problems, yet still forget to take sufficient water each day, take heed of what Cayce told 257–11: "There should be more water taken into the system in a more consistent manner, so that the system—especially in the hepatics and kidneys—may function normally, thus producing . . . correct eliminations of drosses in the system. For there are many channels of elimination from the system, and for this reason each channel should be kept in equilibrium [with the other channels] so that there is not an accentuated condition in any one of the eliminating functions. There should not be an overtaxing of the lungs, liver nor respiratory, but all should be kept in an equal manner.

LACK OF THIS WATER IN THE SYSTEM CREATES AN EXCESS OF SUCH ELIMINATIONS, WHICH SHOULD NORMALLY BE CLEANSED THROUGH THE ALIMENTARY CANAL AND THE KIDNEYS SO THAT DROSSES ARE FORCED BACK INTO THE CAPILLARY CIRCULATION."

In America, the first thing taken into the stomach upon awakening is usually a cup of coffee. In Europe, tea often vies with coffee for this distinction. Coffee addicts, here it comes: "Coffee or tea should not be taken with milk or cream, for this is hard upon the digestion." (5097-1)

Case 816-5 asked if tea or coffee could be used without harmful effects. She was told that: "No one can use them without affecting the body. As to whether they are harmful or not depends upon the extent to which they are used. Use one or the other; don't use them both. Tea is more harmful than coffee. Coffee is a food if it is taken without cream or sugar, and especially without cream; and if taken without caffein . . . it is really a food for the body." [For] "coffee is a stimulant to the nerve system. The dross from coffee is caffein which is not digestible in the system and must necessarily be eliminated. Thus when caffein is allowed to remain in the colon, poisons are thrown off from it. If it is eliminated—it is a food and is preferable to many stimulants that might be taken." (294-86) "While the food values in the milk or cream may be considered of an equal value alone, when used together they form a condition in the lactic juices of the stomach itself that does not make for the proper eliminations carried on through the whole of the alimentary canal." (983-1) "Irradiated or dried milk, as a rule, is much more healthful for most individuals than raw milk." (480-42)

Citrus juices are usually the first thing we think of when deciding what to have for breakfast. They also link themselves in our minds with Vitamin C—although there are many other sources. "C is that from which the structural portions are stored; then drawn upon when it becomes necessary. And when [lack of C] has become detrimental to the body . . . it is necessary to sup-

ply Vitamin C in such proportions as to aid. Else conditions become such that bad eliminations result, because of incoordination
between the excretory functions of the alimentary canal—as well
as functioning of the heart and liver and lungs—through the
expelling of forces that are a part of the structural portion of
the body." (2072-9) [But] "It will be much better if you will
add a little lime with the orange juice and a little lemon with
the grapefruit—not too much, but a little. It will be much better
and act better with the body. For many of these are hybrids, you
see?" (3525-1) What to follow the juice? Certainly not whole
grain cereals, for: "If cereals are taken, do not mix them with
citrus fruits, for this changes the acidity of the stomach to a
detrimental condition. For citrus fruits will act as an eliminant
when taken alone, but when taken with cereals they become as
weight, rather than as an active force in the gastric forces of the
stomach itself." (481-1)

Case 2072-14 asked what food can be used with citrus fruits
to make a complete meal. "Any foods that may be taken at any
time save whole grain cereal."

Case 416-9 wanted to know what should be avoided, and was
given the key to correct diet. *"Rather it is the combination of
foods that make for disturbances with most physical bodies. . . .*
do not eat great quantities of starches with the proteins or meats.
If sweets are taken at the same meal, these are preferable to
starches and meats. Then do not also combine the alkaline-reacting acid fruits with starches." The lunch box will require some
extra creative thinking if we heed the advice given 340-32: "Meat
should not be taken with starches that grow above the ground.
Hence potatoes or potato peelings with meats are much preferable to eating bread with meats . . ." This puts an end to Lord
Sandwich's brainchild: the two slices of bread with a chunk of
meat between them. *"Plenty of lettuce should always be eaten
by almost everybody,* for this supplies an effluvium in the bloodstream that is a destructive force for most of those influences
that attack the bloodstream. It's a purifyer." (404-6)

Lettuce is served too often as a garnish or a bed on which to display other foods. Don't allow it to remain a decoration—eat it! What had Cayce to say of its companion, the tomato?

"Quite a dissertation might be given as to the effect of tomatoes upon the human system. Of all the vegetables, tomatoes carry most of the vitamins, in a well-balanced assimilable manner suitable for the activities in the system. Yet, if these tomatoes are not cared for properly, they may become very destructive to a physical organism. That is, if they ripen after being pulled, or if there is a contamination with other influences or subjects. . . . Nominally, though, tomatoes should form at least a portion of a meal three to four days out of every week, and they will be found most helpful . . .

"The tomato is one vegetable that in most instances . . . is preferable to be eaten after being canned, for it is then much more uniform . . .

"The tomato is among those foods which may be termed non-acid forming." (584-5) ". . . More of the vitamins are contained in tomatoes (vine ripened) than in any other one growing vegetable." (900-386)

In menu suggestions, Cayce gave plenty of raw salads for lunch, usually giving as proportions at least three vegetables which grow above the ground to one which grows below. "Often use the raw vegetables which are prepared with gelatin." (3051-6)

This suggestion was repeated over and over. What is gelatin's secret vitamin? "It isn't the vitamin content but its ability to work with the activities of the glands, causing the glands to take from that absorbed or digested the vitamins that would not be active if there is not sufficient gelatin in the body. . . . There may be mixed with any chemical that which makes the rest of the system susceptible or able to call from the system that needed. It becomes, then, as it were, 'sensitive' to conditions. Without it [the gelatin] there is not that sensitivity." (849-75) "And in the manner of diet, keep away from too much grease or too much of any foods cooked in quantities of grease—whether hog, sheep, beef or fowl! Rather use the lean portions and those meats which will make for body building forces throughout. Fish and fowl are the preferred meats. No raw meat, and very little *EVER* of hog meat—only bacon. Do not use bacon or fats in cooking the vegetables." (303–11)

Case 1710–4 asked for an outline of the proper diet, and things to avoid: "Avoid too many heavy meats, not well cooked. Eat plenty of vegetables of all kinds. Meats taken should preferably be fish, fowl and lamb; others not so often. Breakfast bacon, crisp, may be taken."

However, when choosing vegetables, "have vegetables that are fresh and especially those grown in the vicinity where the body resides. Shipped vegetables are never very good." (2–14)

One might wonder how much this statement reflected the time in which Cayce lived and how valid it might be today. In view of the short time it takes for growing foods to lose their food value after being gathered (see Chapter 6, page 108), and possible laxity in rushing the foods to the consumer due to modern cold storage transportation and newly discovered preserving techniques, it might be even more valid today than it was then. "Do not have large quantities of any fruits, vegetables or meats that are not grown in or come from the area where the body is at the time it partakes of such foods. This will be found to be a good rule to be followed by all. This prepares the system to acclimate itself to any given territory." (3542–1)

Another reason for avoiding the consumption of too much animal flesh is that when we eat, we take into our systems not only the nutritional values of a substance, but also the vibrational pattern of that substance. "The beast of the field of certain natures, that made of certain vibrations brought certain vibrations from within the same system." (900–465) Before taking anything into our system from the animal world, let us think of the animal and decide whether or not we actually want to incorporate its vibrations into our own.

Q. "What should be the diet for this body?"

A. "Not too much of meats of any kind. Rather take fowl, or

fish and vegetables that clarify the blood. These would be cooked onions, beets, carrots, salsify, raw cabbage, celery or lettuce. These will act well with the mental and spiritual forces in the body." (288–9) "Keep away from red meats, ham, or rare steak or roasts. Rather use fish, fowl and lamb." (3596–1)

For those partial to Jewish cooking, Cayce gave his seal of approval to gefilte fish: ". . . Little fish occasionally but none ever fried. Gefilte is well, provided not too highly spiced." (900–383)

Case 5269–1 was told to use the body-building foods such as beef-juice, beef broth, liver, fish, lamb. "All these may be taken BUT NEVER FRIED FOODS."

He ended many readings of dietary suggestions with the words, "never anything fried." These are familiar words to anyone knowing the Cayce readings on diet. There were no mitigations.

"Since onions are supposed to be good for your blood and otherwise, why do they cause such ill-smelling gases?" asked 457–9. "From the most foul at times comes the most beautiful of lilies," was the reply. "Evening (if this is the dinner) the well cooked vegetables, but not those vegetables cooked in or with grease; those cooked in their own juices, as in a steamer or in Patapar Paper. These may be seasoned well with butter, but not seasoned with bacon or with cooking meats of any kind." (844–1)

During Cayce's lifetime, and in the locale in which he lived, it was a practice to cook vegetables to death, literally, and often included in the cooking was a ham hock or hunk of bacon "just to give it flavor." In the light of modern dietary research we know how wrong this way of cooking is, but in those days Cayce was the kitchen pioneer. Steamers are available today which sit inside the cooking pot and prevent the vegetables from touching the water—nothing but the steam gets to them.

Q. "Is it all right to use Club aluminum waterless cooker for preparing my food?"

A. "This is very well, but PREFERABLY Patapar Paper is

the best manner for preparing foods. Of course, there are some foods that are affected in their activity by aluminum,—especially in the preparation of certain fruits, or tomatoes, or cabbage. But most others, it is very well." (1852-1)

Patapar Paper is a cooking parchment—also available today—in which the vegetable is tied, the whole packet then being immersed in a pot of boiling water. The juice of the vegetable apparently is most important. When suggesting the grating of raw carrots into a gelatin salad, he would always warn not to allow the juice to escape, but to put it right into the gelatin.

As to the choice of vegetables, 1968-6 was told to "Keep plenty of those foods that supply calcium to the body. These we would find especially in raw carrots, cooked turnips and turnip greens, and all kinds of salads—especially watercress, mustard greens and the like; these especially taken raw, though turnips greens cooked, but cooked in their own juices and not with fat meats."

Case 462-5's concern for the proper method of cooking foods prompted her question about pressure cookers; she asked if they "destroy any of the vitamins of the vegetables and fruits?" She was assured "No, it preserves rather than destroys them."

However, "All seasoning should be done with butter and salt or paprika (or whatever may be used as seasoning) *after* the foods have been cooked! The cooking of condiments, even salt, *destroys* much of the vitamins of foods." (906-1)

Q. "Does steam pressure cooking at fifteen pounds temperature destroy food values in vegetables?"

A. "No." "[Retention of food values] depends upon preparation, the age and how long since gathered. All these are factors affecting food values. Just as it is so well advertised that coffee loses its value in fifteen to twenty days after its being roasted; so do foods or vegetables lose their food values after being gathered—in the same proportion in hours, as coffee does in days." (340-1)

Surely, this is the strongest argument possible for *anyone* to sprout beans in their kitchens, or even in a hotel bedroom when traveling. It is a perfect way of eating a living fresh food. Bean sprouts are both simple and economical to grow and one of the richest sources of mineral elements which we lack in our daily intake of food that is often merely bulk—or so much dead weight.

A vegetarian needed extra nourishment and was told: "This, to be sure, is not an attempt to tell the body to go back to eating meat. But do supply then, through the body forces, supplements, either in vitamins or in meat substitutes. This is necessary for those who hold to these vegetarian influences." He then went on to say: "But purifying of the mind is of the mind, not of the body. For as the Master gave, it is not that which entereth in the body, but that which cometh out that causes sin. It is what one does with the purpose; for all things are pure in themselves and are for the sustenance of man—body, mind and soul." (5401-1) "Spiritualize those influences, those activities, rather than abstaining. For, as He gave, that which cometh out, rather than that which goeth in, defileth the spiritual body." (295-10)

Should you think that lack of meat will dull the brain—we are assured that "Vegetables will build gray matter faster than will sweets or meats." (900-386)

Although not a great advocate of red meat, as you have probably by now gathered, whenever a body needed strengthening, he would often recommend 'beef-juice'. These are the instructions he gave 1343-2: "Take a pound to a pound and a half of beef, preferably of the round steak. No fat and no portions other than that which is of the muscle or tendon for strength; no fatty or skin portions. Dice this into half-inch cubes, as it were, or practically so. Put same into a glass jar without water. . . . Put the jar into a boiler or container with the water coming to about half or three-fourths from the top of the jar. Put a cloth in the container to prevent the jar from cracking. Do not seal the jar tight, but cover the top. Let this boil (the water with the jar in same) for three to four hours."

Its dosage was explained to 1100-10 in this way: "Take at least a tablespoonful during the day, or two tablespoonsful. But not as spoonsful, rather sips of same. This sipped, in this manner, will work toward producing the gastric flow through the intestinal system."

The value of almonds has already been quoted, but something as simple, and presumably so valuable, cannot be stressed too much: "An almond a day is much more in accord with keeping the doctor away—especially certain types of doctors—than apples. For the apple was the fall (not the almond), for the almond blossomed when everything else died. Remember, this is life!" (3180–3)

Q. What is so great about almonds?

A. "The almond carries more phosphorus and iron in a combination easily assimilated than any other nut." (1131–2)

"Let the iron be rather taken in the foods [instead of medicinally] as it is more easily assimilated from the vegetable forces." (1187–9)

Today, even more than in Cayce's time, we consume large amounts of carbonated drinks. Although there were one or two recommendations favoring them, the majority of times Cayce was strongly against them and referred to them as slops. Case 2157–2 asked if soft drinks were all right "for this body" and was told "No, for very few bodies." "Do not take any form of drinks that carry carbonated waters. The gases of these, as well as all such, are detrimental and only add fire to the unbalanced chemical forces that are segregating themselves in the body." (1013–3)

Case 3009–1 was told point blank, "Do not take carbonated drinks of any kind."

Some real concern appeared when 2461–1 was told that his trouble was brought about by certain disturbances "as well as from that which has been and is a part of the condition by an excess of carbonated forces upon the system itself, combined at times with a toxic condition produced by strong drink." His advice continued with the use of "plenty of water."

His wife wrote a letter to Cayce following this reading in which she said, "You sure were hard on the Coca-Cola, he works for the company and [cutting it out] will be hard to do."

But the Coca-Cola Company need not fear for its continued success.

Case 416–17 was told, "Then do *not* take *any* carbonated drinks—of any nature. Coca-Cola or such are well to clear kidneys, but make same with plain water."

What is the action of Coca-Cola upon the system when taken with plain water? Here are some answers:

". . . will not be harmful, in fact, it would be helpful for the kidneys and for the purifying of the blood flow." (2766–1)

". . . will be beneficial for the body in clarifying or purifying the kidney and bladder disorder." (5218–1)

". . . for this will react with the circulation between the kidneys and the liver and will clear off much of the poisons which will be more beneficial for the activity of the sensory system." (5058–1)

Another important aspect of our diet is the balance we maintain of the acid/alkaline forces. This is most important for when 480–19 asked if immunization against contagious diseases could be set up in any other manner than by inoculations, Cayce gave us a very important key to healthful living. "If an alkalinity is maintained in the system—especially with the lettuce, carrots and celery—these in the blood supply will maintain such a condition as to immunize a person."

How to know what our balance is depends not only upon the food we take into our systems, but by the life we lead governing this intake. "The less activities there are in the physical exercise or manual activity, the greater should be the alkaline-reacting foods taken. Energies or activities may burn acids; but those who lead the sedentary life can't go on sweets or too much

starches . . . these should be well balanced." (798-1) ". . . And
the rest of the diet should consist of the more alkaline-reacting
foods. For, in all bodies, the less activities there are in the physical exercise or manual activity, the greater should be the alkaline-
reacting foods taken.

"Keep an attitude of helpfulness, cheerfulness, hopefulness. Be
optimistic! At least make three people each day laugh heartily,
by something the body says! It'll not only help the body—it'll
help others."

Case 294-86 had a problem with acidity which "is produced
by taking too much sugar in the system in candies and in the
properties which were taken before the stomach was filled with
foods at meals, and then by overloading the system at such times."

"What properties were referred to as being taken into the system before food was taken?" she retorted indignantly. "Candies
and smoking." So there!

There were various aids to digestion which were mentioned,
including antacid tablets and powders, olive oil and a more
sensible diet. One little-known way to help prevent indigestion
is saffron tea: "Just before the meals are taken, drinking that
of a mild tea of Saffron should coat the whole of the stomach
proper. This will aid the digestion." (5545-1)

Directions were given to 2876-1: "Do give the body Yellow
Saffron tea. This is the regular American Saffron. Put a pinch
between three fingers into a crock and pour a pint of boiling
water over same. Let this steep as tea . . . make fresh every day."

The purple thread linking the readings dealing with obesity
was grape juice. This celebrated routine consisted of: "Grape
Juice regularly four times each day, about a half hour before
each meal and before retiring. Use three ounces of pure Grape
Juice . . . with one ounce of plain water, not carbonated water."
(3413-2)

Case 457-8 asked, "Why should the body take grape juice?"
"To supply the necessary sugars without gaining or making for
greater weight." "The grape juice we would keep consistently
to supply the vital forces as in B_4 for the body." (2455-2)

Obesity is still an unsolved riddle to the medical profession.

Usually, the patient is told simply to eat less food and to be more prudent in the choice of diet. Some endocrine glandular concessions are made for certain cases of obesity. However, the thyroid and pituitary can account for only a small percentage of excess body weight. There are many other factors to be considered.

When an obese person consulted Cayce, his obesity was seldom the sole problem. There were other malfunctions—enough to make it impossible to put one's finger on any one cause. Probably the greatest factor contributing to this state was, as Cayce would call it, "an excess of starches in the diet," and following closely on its heels was improper or inadequate eliminations. Several references were made to glandular imbalance, and the lack of coordination between the cerebrospinal and the autonomic nervous system also plays its part—quite an important part—in producing excess body weight.

We are all aware of the various 'crash diets,' of the volumes which have been written on them, greatly publicized by television and in the press. But anyone who has tried one of these crash diets knows that getting one's weight down to normal is not the greatest problem. It is keeping it there.

A beautiful body is the result of perfect health. First the diet must be taken seriously and then the eliminations must be balanced throughout the body. The glandular system must be balanced and any malfunction of the body, *e.g.* nervous system or circulation, must be rectified.

The following advice would be well worth studying by all, regardless of their weight: "Set before self, mentally, that the body would attain. Make it high, and keep the mental self lifted in that direction; for to heal the physical alone, and to have the mental still distorted, would only be the return of the condition when *activities* would be renewed physically. But make the body physically fit, that the body mental may act through same—and make the efforts to bring about that as *is desired*, in a mental and physical body—but make it high! Don't be satisfied with less." (5545-2)

According to Cayce, a whole book could have been written

on the subject of vitamins. Unfortunately it wasn't, but this much was given: "Supply in the vital energies that which ye call vitamins or elements. For, remember, though we may give many combinations there are only four elements in your body: water, salt, soda and iodine. These are the basic elements; they make all the rest! Each vitamin, as a component part of an element, is simply a combination of these other influences—given a name, mostly for confusion, by those who would tell you what to do for a price." (2533-6) "What are those elements in food or drink that give growth or strength to the body? Vitamins? What are vitamins? The Creative forces working with the body energies for the renewing of the body!" (3511-1)

With such power working for the renewing of the body, we might well acknowledge the creative forces by saying a prayer before we take our meals. The real value of saying grace before a meal should be appreciated, for in this way one's attitude becomes one of gratitude and the blessing of the food is a creative act which endows the food with whatever good vibration we transmit to it. In this way you may decide what you would have the food do in your system and still any turmoils you may have brought to the table. "Rest a bit before food or drink is taken. When the body is wrath, mad, or out of temper, or worried—leave food or drink from the system. Never think that either worry or madness may be drowned in drink or in over-feeding the stomach; for these bring distresses to the body." (4124-1)

It must be kept in mind that eating is a way of renewing the body energies and food should be taken in a spirit of joy and harmony or not at all. In a state of harmony one not only receives benefit from the food he takes but from the very atmosphere itself. The atmosphere contains all you expect it to contain. Think about it. There may be limitless treasures invisibly surrounding us, just waiting to be perceived.

One priceless recipe arrived on the wings of a dream. In 1937, Cayce had a dream in which an Egyptian mummy came to life and, after translating certain material for him, gave him a recipe. This dream was questioned later in trance and the same recipe was given. It has since appeared several times in the readings and is known as 'Mummy Food'. "Then follow the regular diets that aid in eliminations. Use such as figs; or a combination of figs and dates would be an excellent diet to be taken often. Prepare same in this manner:

> 1 cup black or Assyrian figs, chopped, cut or ground very fine
> 1 cup dates, chopped very fine
> ½ cup yellow corn meal (not too finely ground)

Cook this combination in two or three cups of water until the consistency of mush. Such a dish as part of the diet often will be as an aid to better eliminations, as well as carrying those properties that will aid in building better conditions throughout the alimentary canal." (2050–1)

Case 4008–1 questioned about "spiritual foods." "These are needed by the body just as the body physical needs fuel in the diet. The body mental and spiritual needs spiritual foods—prayer and meditation, thinking upon spiritual things. For the body is indeed the temple of the living God. Treat it as such, physically and mentally."

There are no shortcuts on the road to good health. Diet is just one of the milestones which must be encountered. A dietary misdemeanor will appear more quickly in the external than any other. So don't be tantalized by anything less than that which is wholesome. Don't build in the present what you will regret in the future. Don't feed your body what it fancies; feed it what it needs.

TONING UP ALL THE RIGHT PLACES

THE NEED for physical fitness is an undisputed fact all over the world. The Olympic games—a tradition started in Greece 2,750 years ago—are still active and draw contestants from all the nations of the world. President Kennedy was sufficiently concerned with the physical fitness of the American citizen to declare a special program. Judging from the enormous number of health spas and gymnasiums in every city, we should be the healthiest race in existence.

Cayce was in complete agreement with need for exercise: "It's well that each body, EVERY body, take exercise to counteract the daily routine activity, so as to produce rest." (416-3) "Common or ordinary understanding should give one the correct idea as to how the application of exercise deals with the body; if a little thought is given to this: That the body is built up by the radiation of vibratory forces from each and every unit of the body functioning in its proper manner.

"Then to overexercise any portion not in direct need of same, to the detriment of another, is to hinder rather than to assist through exercise. Exercise is wonderful, and necessary and little or few take as much as is needed, in a systematic manner. Use common sense, use discretion." (283-1)

From this last statement, it would seem that at the time of this reading, 1927, the exercise consciousness of the populace needed jogging. How true do you think it is today? "There are specific exercises and breathings for the varied activities upon the various organs, the varied activities of the glandular system. These, not too strenuous, are much preferable to outside influences.

For *EVERY* influence for corrective measures is to create within the activating body the awareness of its deficiency or its over- or superfluous activity, and to bring about a *coordinant* condition, a cooperative condition in the body." (903-24)

Let us start with the general exercise suggestions and then look at the specifics.

Case 1206-16, just eighteen years old, asked for *further* suggestions for her best growth and development. Cayce suggested: "The exercises, particularly the setting up exercises, see? These be persistent with daily. Walking is good exercise, all outdoor activities such as tennis, croquet, riding, swimming. All of these are good but a few minutes morning and evening of the setting up exercises, at least three times each week the abdominal exercises." "Of mornings the body should rise early. First take the full setting up exercise of the body, upper and lower, circling the body from the hips up, bending from hips, stooping from hips, circling arms, head and neck." (137-1)

We are all familiar with the head and neck exercise from the chapter which dealt with eyes, but here we have it as part of the regular daily routine and to 481-1 its importance was stressed in the morning and evening: "It would be well that a systematic exercise be taken morning and evening, but don't take it one day and then leave it off for two or three. Take it for three or four minutes morning and evening. In the morning take the exercise of the upper portion of the body, from the waist up, raising and lowering the arms—raising them high above the head, as to scratch—then take the head and neck exercises, and if one is left off, leave off the body *but do not leave off the head and neck exercise.* But take them all! In the evening take the stooping exercise and bending for the lower portion of the body or the swinging of the lower limbs."

In answer to the question "What is the condition of the eyes and what should be done for them?" 417-2 was told after lens correction and lessening of inflammation that "the best stimuli will be an exercise of a circular motion, and of the bending forward, backward and side of head." Our old friend. She then asked what treatment the body should follow to keep physically fit. She was told, "Plenty of exercise in the open and do not overeat."

Posture is also very important. Not only does it keep the organs in their proper position relative to each other, but keeping the spine straight allows all nerve forces to function more normally. It keeps the muscles toned, and projects a far more vital and healthy appearance than slouching.

Specifically for posture, 1773-1 was told: "Mornings upon arising, take for two minutes an exercise in this manner—where the body, standing with the feet flat on the floor, gently rise to the toes, at the same time bringing the hands high above the head. Then bring these as far back as possible or as practical, swinging both arms back. Then gradually bring them toward the front, then let down. Breath IN as the body rises, and OUT as the body brings the hands to the front, slowly. Do this three or four times each morning. This is an excellent exercise for posture." 4003-1 was told: "The best exercise for this body would be to stretch in the manner of a cat, or panther. Stretching the muscles but not straining them causes the tendons and muscles to be put into positions natural for the building of a strong and graceful body."

With his love of balance, Cayce advised 257-167: "These [activities] should be budgeted. Exercise of the mind, as well as exercise of the body in recreational ways and manners. These should be divided, so that there are recuperations . . ."

And he went on to give the green light to handball, tennis, golf and riding.

The mind also needs exercising, as it has a direct reaction to the physical body. When asked what mental exercise would be beneficial, he gave: "Of course meditation is always well—for the mental attitude has much to do with the general physical forces." (2823-2)

"While walking exercise is excellent, these should be more that tends to make for the activity of the feet above the head (lying prone on back, of course), morning and evening, just upon arising and just before retiring and bending back to the shoulders as much as possible. This will be rather severe in the beginning. ... And work the feet much as if pedalling a bicycle, see?" (322-3)

Q. "How much walking should be done daily?"

A. "Whether it is a mile or a step, do that which makes for a better 'feel' for the body; getting into the open." (257-204)

"Keep the exercises as much outdoor as possible, and we will bring the better normal condition for this body." (36-1)

Q. "What type of exercise is best for the body?"

A. "Walking is the best exercise. Bicycling—either stationary or in the open—is well. These are the better types of exercises. The open air activity is better." (2090-2)

And here we have, yet again, a plug for consistency and persistency. "Again let us give: Have a period for recreation, physically. Don't do this one day, or one day a week. If it is not capable of having more than five minutes walk every day, do that! That is better than an hour of strenuous exercise once a month, or even once in a week! There is no better exercise than walking! Not fast, but to be in the open, and to swing the body in the movements—this is well for the body." (257-217)
"Walking is good, especially in the open." [But] "swimming

is better than any. This is good, for the activities of all the muscular forces are brought into play." (920–11)

Case 1154–1 had a golf versus swimming question to which Cayce replied: "Swimming is more satisfactory than golf, though golf in not too strenuous a manner—in that it takes the body in the open more—is very satisfactory. But do not work at it too *hard!* . . . Don't work at golf, play at golf."

There was even a specific exercise for hemorrhoids. To 2823–2 he said: "If this is taken regularly [the exercise], these will disappear of themselves. Twice each day—morning and evening —and this does not mean with many clothes on—rise on the toes, at the same time raising the arms; then bend forward letting the hands go towards the floor. Do this three times each morning and evening. But don't do it two or three times and then quit, but do it regularly each day."

Case 903–6 was pregnant and wanted to know about exercises for the body. "These are as constant developments for any well being, well balanced body. Consistent exercise with conditions as develop. Walking exercise is well . . . yet these [exercises] must ever be consistent with conditions as they arise."

Case 457–9, also pregnant, asked about exercises. She was told: "Those as would be indicated—walking is the best exercise; of course, bending, or the regular setting-up exercises are good."

Case 654–35 had a slight weight problem and was given: "We would take exercises each morning and each evening. These exercises will also aid in keeping a better condition through the bodily forces and reduce that tendency for the increase in weight. Take these same exercises morning and evening for at least five minutes. Do not take them as merely something to be gotten through or gotten rid of, but see, feel, know—by the very activity—that which is being accomplished for the whole system.

"Stand erect, with very little clothing. Rise gently on the toes, at the same time taking a deep breath and raising the hands just as far above the head as possible. Then, still on toes, tend to lean forward, just as far as the body can.

"Keep these up until the body is able to stand on toes and

touch the floor with the tips of fingers. Each time the breath is taken rise on the toes, raising the hands at the same time. Just in the last two of these activities use the head and neck motions also; that is, the head far back, gradually brought forward, turn to the side, circle; or the head and neck exercises, taking the others at the same time."

Case 27–35, the other side of the coin, was too thin. "While there may, with the proper kind of precautions taken, be some little weight added, we would not do this with the use of sweets or too great a quantity of starches. Let it be rather from physical exercise, that might be taken more consistently in a gym or the like."

Overeating, and especially of fat-producing foods, is no answer to adding weight then.

Case 2072–14 wanted a treatment for dryness of hands and skin. She was told to "Use any good oil, as Sweet Oil or such, on the hands and over the body—it will change this. The better change should come from *within* from the better assimilation of that eaten, which will be found to be more improved by the exercises of stretching arms above the head or swinging on a pole would be well. This doesn't mean to run out and jump up on a pole every time you eat, but have regular periods. When you have the activities, do have these exercises, for they will stimulate the gastric flow and let that eaten have something to float in; that is, eat some more!"

As you can imagine, exercises for the abdomen were frequently requested and one was given more often than any other: "The stretching of the abdomen as the exercise with feet against the wall; hands on the floor and raise and circle the body itself. This will keep the abdomen and the hips in correct position and keep body muscles through the hips and abdomen in such condition and positions as to make for much better activity in all the organs of the pelvis, the abdominal area." (1206–16)

When 340–19 asked for an exercise for the muscles of the abdomen she was told: "Let's get them cleansed first! and then we will give you the exercise! Don't try the exercise when you're trying to cleanse them as you'd cause more irritation than you'd be aiding the system."

These 'pelvic rolls' seem to be an almost magical movement. He told 308–13 that they are "an exercise that will strengthen the whole condition of the spine, keep the abdominal muscles well as to general position of the body and keep the limbs in shape as to strengthen the muscles without being detrimental to any portion of the body. . . . This will help the circulation, aid the digestion and improve the general conditions of the body."

Cayce warned that this exercise would not be easy at first; one should start with one movement in each direction to begin, then work up to three times in each direction. He told 5282–1 that it would be good also to reduce arms and calves of legs.

Case 540–11, when she asked for a method of reducing abdomen, was told to "roll on a barrel—this is best!"

Case 417–2's legs felt heavy at times. Asked what would remedy same, Cayce said: "This is produced by impaired circulation through the lower extremities, produced by pressure existent in lower dorsal and lumbars. This may be aided materially by the right character of exercise and by keeping of eliminations as respecting the alimentary canal; exercise being such as takes the blood from the upper portion of the body, distributing same to lower portion, taking time to take specific exercises of stooping, bending and circular motions of mornings of the lower limbs, and then keeping up eliminations. This will correct condition."

Case 412–10's routine was much easier: "Standing flat upon the feet, gently rise upon the toes; do this for some six to eight to ten to fifteen times, gently; at the same time raising the arms gently with same during this, lower portions of the activities. This will. make for the proper circulation through these portions of the body."

For pelvic condition, 4895–1 was told: "Every evening before retiring for three to five minutes, a bending circular motion of the body with the hands on the hips, not bending down, but in circles."

When 369–10 asked what breathing exercises would be best,

she was told: "Those that would be the activity to EVERY well balanced body. Morning and evening exercises with the full and deep inhalation, and quick exhalation from the lungs; breathing in through the nostrils and exhaling through the mouth quickly."

Case 304-3 was told to do "the exercise that will expand the lungs, raising the body at the same time to tiptoes as much as possible, arms extended at right angles from the body."

Yoga-type breathing exercises are practiced by many, and Cayce told 2475-1 that "these exercises are excellent, yet it is necessary that special preparation be made—or that a perfect understanding be had by the body as to what takes place when such exercises are used.

"For BREATH is the basis of the living organism's activity. Thus such exercises may be beneficial or detrimental in their effect upon a body.

"Hence it is necessary that an understanding be had as to how, as to when, or in what manner such may be used."

The breathing exercises, as used in the Yoga teaching, then, are more potent than some realize. For some insight into this, see what Cayce had to say 2745-1 when he asked, "Just what preparation do you advise for the body now?"

"This should be rather the choice of the body, from its OWN development, than from what ANY other individual, entity or source might give.

"Purify the body, purify the mind; that the principle, the choice of ideals as made by the entity may be made manifest.

"Do whatever is required for this—whether the washing of the body, the surrounding with this or that influence, or that of whatever nature.

"As has been experienced, this opening of the centers or the raising of the life force may be brought about by certain characters of breathing—for, as indicated, the breath is power in itself; and this power may be directed to certain portions of the body. But for what purpose? As yet it has been only to see what will happen!

"Remember what curiosity did to the cat!

"Remember what curiosity did to Galileo, and what it did to Watt—but they used it in quite different directions in each case."

The occasions when Cayce advised that we should "see in ourselves" what an exercise, food or any other activity was doing, he was suggesting that we direct the energy—consciously—to do our bidding. Mind is the builder, but what it builds depends upon our own directing of this building force. Choose right now. Do you want to be a Galileo, a Watt, a Renoir—or would you rather be a cat?

CHAPTER *8* *Physiotherapy*

TUNING UP: MASSAGE, BATHS, PACKS

Massage

YOU DON'T have to be sick to enjoy physiotherapy—it could be considered the body tune-up, embracing many techniques and methods. Let us consider one of the pillars of physiotherapy: massage. Apart from its sensual delights, what does it do? and why? "The 'why' of the massage should be considered: inactivity causes many of those portions along the spine from which impulses are received to the various organs to be lax, or taut, or to allow some to receive greater impulse than others. The massage aids the ganglia to receive impulse from nerve forces as it aids circulation through the various portions of the organism." (2456-4)

"Mechanical adjustments"—so often suggested in the readings —are merely the aligning of the spine, along which all our nerve impulses travel. The adjustments activate certain nerve ganglia, attune them to others with which they should have been co-operating and balance the forces of the body. "For as understood by the body and the one that would make the mechanical or osteopathic adjustments, or the massage or the masseuse activity, there is every force in the body to recreate its own self—

125

if the various portions of the system are coordinating and cooperating one with another. Hence the reason why, as we have so oft given from the sources here, that mechanical adjustments as may be administered by a thorough or serious osteopathic manipulator may nearer adjust the system for its perfect unison of activity than most any other means—save under acute or specific conditions and even then the more oft such becomes necessary. Then when such activities and proper precautions are taken, we will find the system is enabled, through these activities—by the proper diet—to assimilate and replenish all those forces that may be supplied through chemical or drug activities." (1158-11)

And again to another individual to explain the benefits of osteopathic adjustments: "As a system of treating human ills, osteopathy is more beneficial than most measures that may be given. Why so? Because in any preventative or curative measures, the condition desired is to assist the system to gain its own normal equilibrium. It is known that each organ receives impulses from other portions of the system, by the suggestive forces—sympathetic system; and by circulatory forces—cerebrospinal system; and the blood supply itself. These course through the system in very close parallel activity, in every single portion of the body. Hence stimulation of the ganglia from which impulses arise (either sympathetically or functionally) must be helpful to the body's efforts toward gaining that equilibrium. (902-1)

In the reading given for 1102-4, Edgar Cayce's patience, love and understanding shone like a beacon. General debilitation was the term used to describe the malaise, and for its improvement was given: "For this body we would have a well balanced diet for better blood and body building . . . with a gentle massage or rub as might be had from a masseuse once a week. These as we find would come nearer to making for the better balance of the body.

"The massage should be given with particular reference to the better drainages from those areas about the upper dorsal and through the cervical areas."

Q. "What local treatment will help correct the difficulty of breathing easily through the nose?"

A. "The massage through the upper dorsal and cervical area, so as to make better drainages toward the normal eliminations; rather than the organs tending toward the exhuming the poisons through the superficial or external activities."

Q. "What local treatment will help correct the 'weeping' condition of the left ear?"

A. "The massage, as indicated, through the head and the neck. For there are those blocks—not lesions but rather sort of blocks in the areas, through the stress and strain under which the body has constantly turned itself recently; and these are affecting principally those areas as indicated, that need the consistent and regular manipulations for the clearing of same."

The dialogue has been given to illustrate much more than the patience which Cayce exhibited. Through it one sees what can result in a body from a kind of self-inflicted stress and strain. The same treatment was suggested for (a) the general debilitated condition, (b) the breathing difficulty and (c) a weeping condition of the left ear. If *ever* stress and strain puts you in a similar position—remember, the message is: MASSAGE.

A compound which was given to 326-5 as a specific for easing her back (neuralgia) has helped so many people since that time that it has become famous as the Strains and Sprains Formula. "This would be a very good specific for backaches, sprains, joints, swellings, bruises, etc.

"To one ounce of Olive Oil add:

> 2 oz. Russian White Oil
> ½ oz. Witch Hazel
> ½ oz. Tincture of Benzoin
> 20 minims. Oil of Sassafras
> 6 oz. Coal Oil (Kerosene)

"It will be necessary to shake this together, for it will tend to separate. But a small quantity massaged in the cerebrospinal system or over the sprains, joints, swellings and bruises will take out the inflammation or pain."

Case 2679-1, aged twenty-four, had badly injured herself, sustaining many cuts and bruises. "And while we would continue the use of the massage with Cocoa Butter, we would alternate this with a massage using three parts Peanut Oil and one part Witch Hazel—which would prevent there being so much scar tissue and less apt for any recurrent conditions from same. While the Peanut Oil and Witch Hazel do not mix, put them in a container sufficiently large to shake them before being poured out to be massaged—all about the areas of those injuries and bruises, and where there have been these. It will not only be soothing but, as indicated, will aid in prevention of further disturbances in the future.

"Alternate these, using Cocoa Butter one time and the Peanut Oil and Witch Hazel combination the next time, see?"

Various compounds were recommended after resting in a good warm bath, others for use after a steam bath or fume. The latter had some substance in the water which was vaporized and introduced to the body in that form. It was suggested that these be given in a cabinet-type sweat bath with the head outside. Inhaling the fumes was not the purpose of the fume bath.

Here are two such formulas:

"To four ounces of NUJOL as the base, add in the order named:

    1 oz. Oil of Pine Needles
    ½ oz. Oil of Pine
    ¼ oz. Oil of Sassafras
    2 oz. Peanut Oil   (303-36)

". . . this combination of oils, added in the order named:

    2 oz. Olive Oil
    2 oz. Peanut Oil

¼ oz. Oil of Pine Needles

¼ oz. Lanolin (liquefied)   (3288-1)

"Should the ingredients separate, shake well before pouring into a saucer into which one can dip the fingers before massaging."

And filed under "circulation: incoordination," "in the order named" was explained: "We would add occasionally the oil rubs in the varied centers; especially from the 8th dorsal to the base of the head in the ganglia, that would produce the better activity by the 'oiling up' of the system—as it were—by absorption and by those things that will make for coordination. Those will be most helpful.

"For the present we would prepare the oil in this manner, in these proportions and in the order as given—for this makes a difference in the way the reactions are upon not only the superficial circulation but the ganglia along the system:

4 oz. Russian White Oil

1 oz. Witch Hazel

1 oz. Olive Oil

1½ oz. Tincture of Benzoin

5 minims Oil of Sassafras

"Shake the solution well together before it is massaged into the cerebrospinal system. Only massage that which will be absorbed by the body; and do this with the fingertips, you see?" (442-5)

Case 263-16 was told to "have every other day, at least, a deep thorough massage along the spine with Peanut Oil; then at times —at least once a week—with an equal combination of Peanut Oil and Oil of Pine Needles. But every other day in the evening, have a thorough massage with the Peanut Oil."

Case 303-27 was also told to take peanut oil rubs along the spine and limbs, but "over the abdominal area and lower portions of the stomach we would massage with an equal combination of Tincture of Myrrh and Olive Oil."

The same formula was given to 298-2 in answer to her question: "What will relieve the tenderness of the skin on my back?"

She was warned to ". . . just gently massage this; do not rub."

Olive oil and cocoa butter were also featured in this enormous cast of ingredients which were given for rubs and massages. Case 307–16 was told to use them "gently" along the spine and "especially over the diaphragm and abdomen thoroughly—especially down the right side and down the left side, but fully across the stomach and diaphragm area—or the upper abdomen. These will be much more beneficial if given thoroughly, regularly using the Olive Oil or Cocoa Butter, or one at a time and the other at the next time."

Case 263–10 was told to have a "gentle massage taken about once a month, as a Swedish massage, would be especially good for this body; first a little sweat produced by a cabinet bath or by being wrapped in a sheet of flannel, and then a THOROUGH MASSAGE with Cocoa Butter AND Olive Oil . . . over the whole body. Massage towards the center of the body always, so that the eliminations may be kept the better."

Peanut oil was given as a rub so often to help alleviate the discomforts of arthritis that it came as quite a surprise to come across these directions for 1224–5, who asked: "How can arthritis of left hip, lower vertebra and hands be lessened?"

"By the applications of healing oils; as the Camphorated Oil, and a combination of Olive Oil and Tincture of Myrrh—equal portions; gently massaged into the area being disturbed. These should be alternated; not one used two or three times and then the other two or three times, but each day alternate; using the Camphorated Oil one time; the combination of Olive Oil and Tincture of Myrrh the next time, see?"

Case 630–3 had glaucoma and was instructed to have a thorough massage each day, preferably of an evening when ready to retire, as *part* of the total plan. It was not something to be hurried, or "gotten through with" as he told so many people when advising treatments. The massage was to be given from the base of the brain (or first cervical) to the ninth dorsal along the spinal system.

"The oils would be combined in this manner: to four ounces of Russian White Oil, or Usoline, as the base, add—in the order named:

    1 oz. Peanut Oil
    ½ oz. Oil of Cedar Wood
    ¼ oz. Oil of Sassafras Root
    ¼ oz. Lanolin (dissolved)

". . . just what the body will absorb."

Specifically for dermatitis, 513-2 was given, as an adjunct to other treatments, an oil massage given with an "equal combination of Olive Oil, Tincture of Myrrh and Tincture of Benzoin. . . . Massage this combination especially in the joints of the body; knees, feet, across the hips, up the spine . . . upward. Massage gently all the body will absorb each evening . . ."

Case 845-10, in her menopause, was told that "occasionally a good rubdown or massage would be helpful with special reference to the areas from the ninth dorsal downward; especially, though just as a rub and a rather DEEP massage, following a mild sweat."

The size and shape of a woman's breasts can have a great deal to do with the way she faces the world: her confidence, self-esteem as a woman, in fact, her whole attitude. We are seldom satisfied with ourselves and because of this we feel that if only this or that were changed, all around us would change. Sometimes the desired change is possible through a surgical face lift, sometimes rhinoplasty—or 'nose job.' Plastic surgery is also performed on the breasts these days; the insertion of special material in the form of pads, or injections of silicone substance, and sometimes, a nip and a tuck.

Q. "What can be done to develop the bust to offset the angular line of my body?"

A. "Massaging the mammary glands with Cocoa Butter; not the bust but the glands. Massage always upward, not down, not around but upward. This means commence at about the waistline under the arms, especially the patches where there are the mammary glands, and where the emunctory patches supply nutriment to the glands." (3376-1)

Case 2185-4's shoe was on the other foot.

Q. "How can the breasts be reduced, harmlessly, to a more normal size . . . ?"

A. "By bathing the areas of the glands in a medium strength alum water and massaging with Camphorated Oil . . . the area of the mammary gland; that is from which they drain or are sustained in their circulation. Rub away from the breast—under the arm and down the side of the body—around the outer areas, and we will see a change."

For 607-1 he gave: "For the mammary glands and around the breast, to make them more firm and not so large, we would massage a compound into the glands prepared in this manner:
"To two ounces of Cocoa Butter (dissolved) add: Oil of Butterfat, forty minims; Alum Water (almost a saturated solution), ten minims. Stir this well together. Once or twice a week massage the glands around the arms and around the lower portion of the breast, upper portion and massage thoroughly around the edge—will make these more firm."

Q. "Is there anything that can be done to reduce the bust?"

A. "There has been given a lotion through these sources, an almost perfect lotion for such, that does not injure, does not deter from any activity save as respecting the size or the condition of the bust." (275-37)

The lotion to which he was referring was given to 903-18. Its formula follows: "To four ounces of heated Olive Oil, add (melted) a level teaspoonful of Cocoa Butter, with 50 (fifty) minims of a saturated solution of alum water."
He then continued directions for its use. "This that has been

given should be massaged on the glands and the muscles about same, rather than on the bust itself; for the size, the character of same, is produced by the glands' activity from the system."

The versatility of cocoa butter can be used to extricate us from other predicaments. Case 5188-1 seemed to have a magnetic attraction for mosquitoes and to overcome this was instructed to "occasionally, massage along the spine with Cocoa Butter; that is an ounce in which there has been put five grains of quinine, mix thoroughly. Massage this along the spine, under the arms and in the groin. Not only will the mosquito not bite, but there will be no malaria. These are not as an omen, but are those influences which will keep the body in attune with the infinite." *

Baths
Physiotherapy is a mixed bag of tricks, sometimes used one at a time, but more often in conjunction with each other. Cayce's suggestions for baths were nearly always followed by a shower and a rub or massage. The suggestions included the dry heat baths, steam baths and fume baths. Witch hazel was a frequent suggestion. "About twice a month . . . we would have a cabinet sweat and fume bath; not heavy sweats in the dry heat, but preferably with fumes of Witch Hazel. Follow this by a thorough rub, using an equal combination of Pine Oil and Peanut Oil." (1968-3) "We would take systematically, a series of hydrotherapy treatments. Each treatment should include a dry heat bath followed by the fumes with same of Witch Hazel; then the hot and cold shower, or needle shower; then the thorough rub down—a massage of the body with Pine Oil (preferably for this body)." (3000-1)

The reading for 1276-1 gave an explanation of the properties of the ingredients: "Steam or vapor baths—combining Witch Hazel and the Oil of Pine, or Oil of Pine Needles and Witch Hazel—will make for purifying, strengthening, cleansing of the body and skin. Such a bath would be taken once a week, or

* Author's note: In 1949, Dr. Frank Moeser of Pemberville, Ohio, reported to the ARE that he used the mosquito repellent with 100 percent success.

after a bit, once a month; with a thorough rub-down following same, with a massage or masseuse activity over the whole body."

Another combination of ingredient fume bath was given for 2957-1: "In the hydrotherapy treatment should be included a good sweat, not with dry heat but rather the fume bath cabinet sweat; for the dry heat would be too draining on the body. For the fumes, use an equal combination of Witch Hazel and Rose-water, or a teaspoonful of each in a pint of water that would form vapor to settle over the body, see?"

"To cleanse these [rashes] we would use first, every third day, take the vapor baths and in the vapor as is created for same let there be that of the Oil of Sassafras applied in same. To the half pint of water (this as proportion) add ten minims, or drops, of the Oil of Sassafras. After this is taken there should be the thorough rub-down over the whole system of the body with a coarse towel, or cloth, to get a stimulation to the capillary cir-culation." (4557-1)

Sometimes a more active medicinal property was added to the fumes. 288-23 was told: "Sweats (steam baths) would be good for this (bringing better conditions)—provided Iodine is used in the sweats or in the water. Not over five to eight minutes at first, gradually increasing. . . . Do not take such sweats with-out first taking three to four glasses *full* of water."

At times he simply advised, "At least twice each week, have those sweat cabinets, with a thorough rub-down afterwards." (2096-1)

Should you ever have occasion to have a steam bath, prefera-bly followed by a delicious massage, remember to luxuriate in it. Do not get dressed immediately afterward to run out in the open air. Try to rest awhile, to allow the body to adjust itself to the stimulation and fully absorb the oil chosen for use as the 'medium for the massage.'

Packs
The stack of cards in the files at the library of the ARE head-quarters in Virginia Beach under 'Packs' is thick enough to sup-ply material for a volume or two on this subject alone. The

range of packs includes ice—for reducing swelling among other things; grapes—to reduce fevers and draw toxins; mullein; salt —hot and cold; onions; potatoes; mud; sand; epsom salts; Glyco- Thymoline; castor oil; witch hazel; hog lard; mutton tallow with turpentine and camphor; etc.

In this section we shall just pick some interesting packs at random.*

Pure apple cider vinegar and iodized table salt were the ingredients for a pack—or massage in a saturated solution—for strained ligaments and bruises. For an ankle injury: ". . . applying whenever the pain is severe in the lumbar and sacral region, and in any portion of the limb (for it changes), those properties of saturated Salt and Apple Vinegar, heated as hot as the body can bear." (49–1)

Should you return home from the country somewhat earlier than your doctor, with a souvenir from a malevolent mosquito or other hungry insect try "this application over the bite and swelling. Moisten salt or make it wet with Turpentine and put on as a poultice, not binding. Change this every hour or so until most of the swelling is gone." (2015–9)

Should the little one incur some abrasions while playing, remember the advice given to 3918–2. She was told that the best thing to put on hers "would be the Mullein Stoops, *preferably* the green, though if this is not available the dry may be used." To make the mullein stoops, one simmered (not boiled) the leaves in water for a few minutes and then applied the hot water —with the leaves.

Case 1112–8 asked how to help a bloodshot eye and was told that "the applications of hot water with Camphor poured on packs that would be put on the side of the head and temple, these will tend to relieve the distress and take away the blood- shot condition."

Q. Why on the side of the head and not on the eye itself?

A. "About the eyes and face use any good astringent; as flan-

* Author's note: Mud packs have been covered in Chapter 2.

nelette or cotton cloth dipped in Witch Hazel, applied to the back of the head, across the side of the face—not directly in the frontal portion, but to those areas from which that portion of the eyes receives its impulse." (243–34)

Epsom Salt packs, which are far from new, were used for a number of reasons. 3281–2, suffering from arthritis was told to treat "on the knees with heavy packs of Epsom Salts until these are made to be very hot so that there will be the breaking up of the accumulations there."

And 5700–9, whose problem was dysmenorrhea (painful menstrual periods): "Would be well that the body apply hot packs, especially of a saturated solution of Epsom Salts, across the small of the back, or across that portion where the pain and misery is."

Case 2585–2 had the same problem. Cayce told her that "there are times when there is a great deal of disturbance and stress, just at and through the periods.

"At such times, apply Glyco-Thymoline packs over the ovarian area, or over the ovaries both right and left. Use three to four thicknesses of cotton cloth saturated with Glyco-Thymoline. Apply Salt heat over same. Heat salt and put it in a bag that may be used as a pack."

Glyco-Thymoline packs were recommended for various uses including packs of same for periods of an hour to an hour and a half long the day before making mechanical adjustments—to relax the areas to be adjusted. At times warm packs were suggested over newly healed injuries, sometimes in conjunction with salt and vinegar (used alternately). In cases of arthritis they were prescribed to relax the trouble spots.

"The body will rest better and it will respond more to the treatments as the massages are given." (849–71)

Glyco-Thymoline packs were even recommended for cysts which were due to "accumulations into pockets in the lymph circulation." "For these . . . we would apply a poultice of Glyco-Thymoline, as a pack using three to four thicknesses of gauze thoroughly moistened and applied to these cysts—warm, not hot but warm. Change the applications every twenty minutes, doing this for about an hour." (2957–1)

Castor oil packs affect the lymphatic system of the body, and their many benefits are still being discovered. They were recommended whenever lesion or adhesion obstruction hindered the normal flow of the body. All readings given for cholecystitis (gallstones) included castor oil packs as part of the overall plan.

How to apply a castor oil pack: "Have at least three to four thicknesses of old flannel saturated thoroughly with Castor Oil. Then apply on this, an electric pad. Let this get just as warm as the body can stand—cover with oilcloth to prevent soiling linens." (5186-1)

In this modern age, people are discovering that disposable diapers are useful for many things other than babies. Although the purists will shudder, try one over the soaked old flannel. It certainly makes it easier to handle and catches the extra drips.

Q. Where do the packs go?

A. "Over the gall duct area and extend to the caecum down the right side, and across the abdomen." (5186-1)

Case 1523-15 was planning on motherhood and wanted to know if "the continuing of castor oil packs for dissolving adhesions would interfere with pregnancy or tend to eliminate impregnation." "Rather it would be advisable to use same, that when there is pregnancy it would prevent a great deal of distress and anxiety."

Case 3492-1 was told to "apply the packs warm, sufficient to make for that radiation of activity to the body, and then apply the electric pad—that throughout the whole body there may be that radiation which brings elimination of poisons from the body."

Miracles have been performed since the beginning of time. The Bible is full of their records. The miracles Moses performed in Egypt were a prelude to his parting of the Red Sea. Jesus performed miracle after miracle—and His promise was that we could do all that He did and greater. When the white man first appeared to the American Indian with his 'match box' and 'fire stick,' it must have seemed miraculous. What constitutes a miracle? Surely when anything happens, the workings of which we are ignorant, it appears miraculous. There are some who think that spring and the blooming anew each year of trees and plants is a miracle. No small miracle among these is the palma Christi, from which we get castor oil.

CHAPTER *9* *Eliminations*

A VARIETY OF METHODS
FOR INNER CLEANSING

WHEN ELIMINATIONS are less than perfect, the natural flow of the body is hampered and cannot function to its maximum efficiency. We have all at times felt "one degree under," if not more than one degree. Chances are, if the reason for this malaise stemmed from bodily causes, it would be from faulty eliminations.

While making a study of the Edgar Cayce readings dealing with physical problems, it became very clear that faulty eliminations are at the base of nearly every dis-ease. If they are not the sole cause, they are certainly one of the contributing factors. Following are some random extracts chosen to show the wide range of effects which Cayce attributed—completely or in part—to faulty eliminations.

Appendicitis
"There is, as we find, an engorgement in the colon area also. This has been the basic disturbance; producing a *pressure.*"*
(1194-1)

* Author's note: Italicized words indicate specific activities or systems affected by imperfect eliminations.

Allergies (hives)
". . . through the *sympathetic system,* as well as those of the dis-
tributions in the eliminating system; so that we have such
hindrances as is manifested in the eliminations, especially as
seen in the *skin.*" (1734–4)

Laryngitis
"First, in the *blood supply*–here we find the conditions are an
overtaxed blood supply, through the manner in which eliminations have been carried on in the system. This leaving drosses,
especially in the alimentary canal, affecting directly the liver
and this re-infection . . ." (191–1)

Athlete's foot
". . . we have a *lack of coordination* between the eliminating systems of the body . . ." (412–11)

Vertigo
"All this [languidness, dizziness] is produced by the *conditions
in the pelvis and lower intestines.*" (294–3)

Baldness
"Keep the eliminations better in the body and we will find the
circulation will be improved." (2653–2)

Halitosis
"This [the body] we find good in many respects—yet lacking in
the ability to produce the *perfect eliminations through the lower
portions of the system.*" (4420–1)

Headaches (migraine)
"These, as we find, arise from a condition that exists through
the alimentary canal, especially as part of *the circulation in the
colon.*" (5052–P–1)

Bursitis
"As we find, there are the acute conditions of neuritis; and a

combination of disturbances arising from pressures in the colon.
Though the disturbance is in the bursa and the arm of the
shoulder, the source of this arises from a colon distress." (340-47)

Arteriosclerosis
"Now, as we find, there are very definite conditions that disturb
the better physical functioning of this body; and these have to
do with the eliminations in the body." (506-1)

Arthritis
"In the *pathological conditions* that are active *in the mind and
the body* there is a lacking of proper eliminations." (3363-1)

Skin (complexion)
". . . for these are as but those *eliminations* in system being
thrown out *in improper directions.*
   "As is seen also from pores that appear to be large, or blackheads, or spots appearing in portions of the skin." (1101-3)
   Has the point been made? If one had to find the physical
culprit most commonly causing bodily disease, it would surely
have to be imperfect eliminations.
   Elie Metchnikoff, a Russian-born French scientist,* did much
research on gerontology. He is most famous for his work on
intestinal flora. His investigations of the human body, its function and pitfalls, led him to the realization of the concentration
of toxins produced and kept in the colon. The colon is about
five feet of tubing, not smooth like a garden hose, as many sup-
pose, but having many hiding places along its length where
fecal matter can become imbedded and remain for an indefinite
period. ". . . and there is the tendency for the accumulations
through the colon, this makes for some of the cells or pockets in
same to at times carry for too great a period those fecal forces
that become irritating and heavy." (843-2)
   Constipation, or even incomplete evacuations, can allow the
reabsorption by the system of poisons which it has previously

---

* Author's note: Metchnikoff was born in 1845 and died in 1916.

(in a normal state) successfully filtered. Metchnikoff realized this and called his discovery autointoxication.

Although Metchnikoff's gerontological studies were vast in scope, he is remembered mainly for his recommendation of Lactobacillis Bulgaricus—yogurt—to counter autointoxication. This is often referred to as "planting friendly flora" in the colon.

Edgar Cayce's many references to yogurt and fresh buttermilk covered cases of diabetes, general debilitation, asthenia, obesity, arthritis, appendicitis tendencies, duodenal ulcers, cancer, asthma, toxemia, tubercolosis, cysts, colitis, anemia, and of course assimilations and eliminations.

Although the complete treatments for the following individuals were in most cases extremely lengthy and complex, sometimes requiring follow-up or check readings, the inclusion of the use of buttermilk or yogurt as an adjunct in the diet was often stressed.

Toxemia
"Use yogurt in the evening meal. This is to act as a cleanser for the alimentary canal, as well as a better balance for the fermenting and eliminations of poisons from the system." (1762-1)

Assimilations and eliminations
"Any form of yeast or yogurt for the body will be well. Of course this is a portion of that as will be had from buttermilk. It is those germicidal influences in same that will be effective upon the intestinal system." (538-57)

Asthma
"At the evening meal there may be also taken buttermilk, if fresh, or the Bulgarian milk. These would be well." (5682-2)

Cancer
"Do not eat meats of any great quantity. Plenty of buttermilk." (1967-1)

Tuberculosis

"Do use . . . the combination found in yogurt . . . as an antiseptic for the intestinal tract. Take this regularly." (3154-1)

Eliminations

"Noons, we would take, between this meal and the evening meal, either the Bulgarian milk or those of the lactic acids in milk, or those as are combined in yogurt, see?" (1186-3)

Diabetes

"Let plenty of buttermilk be taken at one of the meals each day, you see; for this (preferably fresh buttermilk) carries in same those properties that would aid in creating that effluvium that is preferable to be in the intestinal system under the existent conditions." (2040-1)

Asthenia

"As much buttermilk as the body will assimilate will always be good for the system." (67-1)

A favorite way to purifying the system, especially among those familiar with Cayce readings, is the apple diet. This diet is not recommended for weight loss; its purpose is solely to detoxify the system, although some weight loss should be expected due to the lack of food intake. "We would use first the apple diet to purify the system; that is, for three days eat nothing but apples of the Johnathan variety if possible. This includes the Delicious which is a variety of the Johnathan. The Johnathan is usually grown farther north than the Delicious, but these are of the same variety, but eat some. You may drink coffee if you desire, but do not put milk or cream in it, especially while you are taking the apples. (780-12)

"This [the apple diet] is to cleanse the activities of the liver, the kidneys, and the whole system—where there has been disturbance.

"On the evening of the third day of the apple diet, take internally half a teacupful of Olive Oil!

"Then, after that do not overgorge the system when beginning to eat again. Have rather a normal diet, but not too rich nor too highly seasoned foods.

"Be active in the open, but *not* so as to overstrain the body during the period of . . . the apple diet." (1850-3)

"No raw apples; or if raw apples are taken, take them and NOTHING else—three days of raw apples only, and then Olive Oil and we will cleanse ALL toxic forces from ANY system!" (820-2)

Mono-diets give the organs a chance to rest. Although apples appeared to be Edgar Cayce's preferred choice of food for a purifying mono-diet, he also recommended a diet of only citrus fruits (oranges with lemons) or grapes (pitted, of course). (1498-1) The orange diet was recommended for five days, the grape for four, the apple for three. Apples seem to work faster. "But after EITHER of these—that is, on the last day of such a diet—take a half teacupful of Olive Oil. This would cleanse the system from the impurities, preventing the inclinations for gas formation and for this regurgitation that is taking place in the lower portion of the duodenum." (1713-21)

As for the amount of apples recommended: "But don't go without the apples—eat them—all you can—at least five or six apples each day. Chew them up, scrape them well. DRINK PLENTY OF WATER, and follow the three-day diet with a big dose of Olive Oil." (1409-9)

He also recommended that she take a series of the castor oil packs before taking the apple diet, but he warned her that they must not run concurrently. "First one, THEN the other."

The amounts of olive oil varied from one tablespoonful to half a cup (the latter being the more frequent). Although 780 was told to take her olive oil on the morning after the diet, it was generally advised to take it on the evening of the third day.

One twenty-six-year-old, 567-7, was concerned about having a tapeworm. Cayce recommended the apple diet as a way of testing herself for tapeworms. "And this would remove fecal matter that hasn't been removed for some time! But it will certainly indicate there is no tapeworm."

At twice-yearly intervals, many present-day ARE members take a three-day series of castor oil packs followed by a three-day apple diet. Quite a number of ARE study groups in New York City have made the apple diet a group activity. Each participant takes a series of castor oil packs for three days prior to eating the apples, and celebrates the end of the whole affair by spending a day in the country communing with nature.

Another means of detoxification was colonic irrigations, which in their last peak period of popularity were often badly administered or taken in excess by the overzealous. "Well that every colon be cleansed *occasionally* with the colonic irrigations." (843-2)

Edgar Cayce interchanged the terms hydrotherapy and colonic irrigations. "For hydrotherapy and massage are preventative as well as curative measure. The cleansing of the system allows the body forces themselves to function normally and thus eliminate poisons, congestions, and conditions that would become acute throughout the body." (257-1)

But here is a proviso well worth noting: "They (colonics) are seldom curatives, UNLESS there are those measures taken to aid in correcting the cause of the disturbance." (303-34)

Diet was always stressed by Cayce as an important adjunct to physiotherapeutic measures. "This [cleansing] may be done in NO BETTER MANNER THAN BY HAVING COLONIC IRRIGATIONS OCCASIONALLY and by including in the diet such things as figs, rhubarb and the like. Hydrotherapy and physical exercise . . . should bring the better conditions for this body. These are the manners in which the body, OR ANY INDIVIDUAL BODY, may keep better activities." (4003-1)

Asked how often colonics should be administered, he gave: "This depends on how often they are needed. These are things that are used as aids. . . . When there is the lack of eliminations through the alimentary canal, then to cleanse the colon, have the irrigation. Whether this is necessary once a week, twice a week, once in six weeks or once in six months depends upon the manner in which the body treats itself." (303–34)

How do you treat yourself in the total physical picture? Do you make a fetish of one aspect of healthful living such as exercise and weekly visits to the health spa—and follow this by a dinner of hot dogs, French fries and pastries? Or obversely, do you make it a point to eat "all the right things" and then allow them to become drosses to the system for want of exercise?

The effectiveness of hydrotherapy depends upon its perspective in the total picture. Never rely on the colonic as a cure-all. It is only one balance point on the tightrope we walk to health and beauty. "But these are well to be used when needed. If they are given body temperature with the water used, and the cleansing solutions in same, the Salt and Soda in proportions indicated, and the Glyco-Thymoline as the purifyer or the like—these will not be weakening but will help. But too often given, too hot or too cold water, they will be disturbing." (303–31) The proportions of the cleansing solutions were: "In the first waters, use Salt and Soda in the proportions of a heaping teaspoonful of Table Salt and a level teaspoonful of Baking Soda (both) thoroughly dissolved—this added to each half-gallon of water.

"In the last water use Glyco-Thymoline as an intestinal antiseptic to purify the system in the proportions of a tablespoonful to the quart of water." (1745–4)

"It would be well that the Glyco-Thymoline, or more of the Soda or Salt—weak solution—be used, that act as an antiseptic for the body; for while it is well to keep an irritated place *clean,* too much activity brings too much accumulation of the mucomembranes' activity that produces irritation or soreness." (279–10)

Case 3104-1 was told "to take three drops of Glyco-Thymoline in water before retiring at night . . . the Glyco-Thymoline acts as an intestinal antiseptic of an alkaline nature."

"Take small quantities—eight to ten drops—of an intestinal antiseptic, such as seen in that of Glyco . . ." (99–5)

"Use an alkalizer for the alimentary canal. Take three to four drops of Glyco-Thymoline internally in a little water each day. Do this for a period sufficient to get the odor of Glyco-Thymoline in the stool. This will purify the whole of the alimentary canal and create an alkaline reaction through the lower portions of the alimentary canal." (1807-3)

One fringe benefit of this alkalinity is the knowledge that the common cold "cannot, does not exist in alkalines." (808-3) If your system is inclined toward colds and congestion, bear this in mind.

"In keeping these, then, we will find that we will also aid in keeping a balance through eliminations.

However, as it is necessary to rinse the mouth, as it is necessary to wash the hands, it may be found just as necessary to cleanse the colon. This should be done with enemas when necessary to keep a normal balance, and which prevents accumulations of forces or influences that would cause the excesses which the emotional or general forces of the body itself may not take care of. But let there be eliminations each day through the alimentary canal. This should be taken (such an evacuation or enema) at the temperature of the body, and be sure that there are salines or salt in same; teaspoonful to a quart and a half of water, and occasionally a level teaspoonful of soda combined with same. These will *not* produce irritations; these will not cause disturbances or prevent the *natural* influences or forces of elimination but tend to create through the usage of same the strong, *healthy* activity of the walls of the alimentary canal—and to create a better, more equalized or balanced movement even from the duodenum throughout the entire length of the alimentary canal." (1276-1)

This will surely answer any questions which might have been lying dormant about the frequency one should expect for evacuation.

Q. "Do you advise the use of colonics?"

A. "When these are necessary, yes. For everyone, everybody,

should take an internal bath occasionally, as well as external baths. People would be better off if they would." (440-2)

Colonics are "aids," as Edgar Cayce puts it, and their frequency should be indicated by the need. The better way would be to construct one's life habits to make the need of aids a rare resort. "For those conditions that have become rather as habits, and those tendencies or necessities for the body to use eliminants —or those things that tend to make for the flow of the gastric forces or the peristaltic movement through the intestinal system (for we find much of this is habit, AND the body, the system has come to depend upon cathartics), we would create for the system that which will cooperate in making for better coordination with the adjustments and treatments as indicated. Then, we would give these—in this way and manner . . .

"Then *make* for self a regular period, after the morning meal, for the evacuation or for going to stool, see? Let this be as habit. Let this be taking the place of the cathartics and the like." (777-3)

Q. "Should anything be taken for eliminations?"

A. "*Correct your eliminations better by diet* than by taking eliminants, when possible. If not possible to correct otherwise, take an eliminant . . . but these elimination problems will be bettered if a great deal of the raw vegetables are used and not too much of meat; but do eat fish and fowl and lamb occasionally . . . don't fry it." (3381-1)

"Set up better eliminations by the use of those foods that tend to set up better drainages . . . laxative foods such as a great deal of black figs and the white and the purple also, and the prunes and prune preparations." (3336-1)

The eliminants given were varied; the following extracts will give some choices. The most mentioned laxative in the readings was Fletcher's Castoria. "Now to cleanse the system, we would set up eliminations with Castoria." (2752-3)

"We would give the Castoria in broken doses, ten to twelve drops every half hour until there are thorough eliminations." (2824-6)

"Better conditions are brought about by taking this in small quantities and often, you see; about half a teaspoonful every half hour." (1541-9)

Fidelity to one eliminant is not the order of the day. Despite the frequency of recommendation of Castoria, note: "Rather than so much of the Castoria in the present—for this can become irritating, of course—we would occasionally change to other eliminants. As we have indicated to other bodies, it is well to alternate these rather than continuing to take just one type of eliminant." (264-56)

"For a laxative take Senna Leaf (or Senna Pod) tea, using four or five of the leaves placed in an empty cup and then pour hot water on it and let stand for thirty to forty-five minutes; strain and drink it. Do this about once a week and it will be good for the body, as it does not become habit-forming and is a correct laxative for most individuals—though not everyone." (457-14)

"For the eliminations generally, we would use Zilatone as an activity upon the eliminating system, so that the organs of the system may be cleansed throughout." (1523-1)

"Eno Salts is the best laxative for *this* body, for this is of the fruit and not the mineral. . . . should be taken in small doses, almost every day for a period of a week at a time and it will be most beneficial." (462-4)

"We would use a saline laxative to make for better alkalization of the whole system . . . Sal Hepatica." (2526-2)

"Mineral rather than the vegetable eliminants, especially such as may be found in Upjohn's Citrocarbonates." (2051-7)

"And keep in your routine occasionally a dose of Upjohn's Citrocarbonate and Milk of Magnesia, not both the same day, no. But once or twice a week take each of these, or one or the other of these." (618-2)

"If there is the insistent non-activity of eliminations as well as should be, the taking of small quantities of Olive Oil with the activities of the system, would be preferable to taking Yeast or Cathartics or the like. We would take about half a teaspoonful of the Olive Oil—about three to four times each day, when it is taken. This will not only supply nutriment to the digestive tract but will aid in the eliminations and is an intestinal food." (1622-1)

Castor oil packs have been recommended time and again for intestinal impactions and adhesions, as well as setting up all manner of activities. Specifically for eliminations: "Begin with the use of Castor Oil Packs an hour each day for three days. Use at least three thicknesses of flannel, lightly wrung out of the Castor Oil, as hot as the body can stand it and applied over the liver and the whole of the abdomen, especially upon the right side of same. Keep the packs warm by using an electric pad. After the third day of using the packs, take a high enema to relieve the tensions throughout the colon and lower portions of jejunum, using a colon tube for same." (2434-1)

"We would apply hot Castor Oil Packs continuously for two and a half to three hours. Then have an enema, gently given." (1523-9)

The following was given to one soul, 3078-1: "If there is not the entire elimination, just as breaking self from any other habit —if ye break over, try again! In the try, help will come. In the application there may be established the knowledge of the truth and the way, and help may come physically, mentally, spiritually. For, if ye know the truth—and apply it not—it is sin. And if sin lies at thy door, can ye have peace with self or with others?"

How many of us, knowing what to do, always act upon what we know? Case 3051-7 asked, "Since all disease is caused by sin, exactly what causes the colon and elimination condition I have?" and was told, "The sin of neglect. Neglect is just as much sin as grudge, as jealousy. Neglect!"

In the readings, assimilations were usually linked with eliminations of the body. The following information was given to 311-4, suffering from psoriasis: "These disturbances have to do with assimilations and the eliminations of the body. There should be a warning to ALL as to such conditions; for would the assimilations and the eliminations be kept nearer normal in the human family, the days of life might be extended to whatever period desired. For the system is builded by the assimilations of that which it takes within—and it is able to bring resuscitation SO LONG AS THE ELIMINATIONS DO NOT HINDER."

Eliminations, however, are not concerned solely with the colon. 302-9 was told "more rest, better eliminations—not merely through the alimentary canal, but coordination of eliminations."

Even your best friend won't tell you. But Cayce would—and did. Case 4073-1 was inquiring about a skin condition. After being told about the incoordination of his systems of elimination, Cayce added: ". . . and thus through the perspiratory and respiratory system—there is the bad breath also. There are the poisons eliminated that should be eliminated through the alimentary canal. Thus the rash."

"How can I get rid of bad breath?" asked 5198-1. "By making better conditions in the eliminations. Take Glyco-Thymoline as an intestinal antiseptic. Two or three times a day put six drops of Glyco-Thymoline in the drinking water.

"This is a condition of poisons being thrown off into the lungs [into the body forces] from the changing in cellular activity [or through the body] of lymph forces that become fecal."

We are told via the advertising media that bad odors from the body are offensive. We are gradually being persuaded to clog the glandular activity in not only the under-arm area, but also the groin area. We are told that unless we use one of a number of mouthwashes two or three times a day, we are in danger of losing our friends, jobs and loved ones. Even the candies we eat must contain deodorizing agents to insure that one stolen kiss will lead to another.

When the eliminatory systems of the body are coordinated, offensive odors need not be feared. Should one become apparent, look to the cause and correct it. A mouthwash or a lozenge cannot compensate for a smoothly acting bodily function.

However we view it, we cannot deny that the elimination of poisons from our systems is one of the foundations of a healthy body. There is so much reference made to eliminations that it behooves us to try to outline some rules of thumb on which to base our decisions. Rules are ever guidelines only. For every rule made, a way to break it can be found. But, in the long run, who is being cheated? If something feels right to you, go along with it. If it feels wrong, discordant, it may not be right *for you*.

Discover your enemy and choose your weapons.

Part III

THE TOTAL BEING

THE THIRD and final part of our book, which is a quest for beauty —a *possible* quest—deals with subjects which might be termed 'metaphysical.' What does this mean? Simply, beyond the physical. One might say, one step ahead, or above. You might picture it as being on a different vibrational plane; it is a realm which cannot be proved scientifically in the physical; only by its fruits may you know it. But these fruits are plentiful. Considering that we are 'using' the channel, Edgar Cayce, to reach a source of knowledge to aid us in this quest for beauty, it is not out of character for this book to introduce many influences. All that is asked of you is that you accept these offerings of information with an open mind, if they are not already familiar to you, and judge them by their fruits. See if—and how—they can work for you.

THE CULMINATION OF MANY ATTEMPTS

"FOR THINE own soul seeks expression," said Cayce. Now that we have beautified the body, let us explore the importance of the soul and its vitality to the whole person, "expressing that which may bring to self, to others, first of all CONTENTMENT; for upon this is peace, harmony, happiness attained." (541-1)

Knowing our reason for being in the earth can make the experience in this lifetime more meaningful and bring a sense of contentment, that secret ingredient manifested in the smile of the Mona Lisa.

In order to come to a deeper understanding of ourselves and realize new dimensions of our relationship to the whole, certain pieces, as in a jigsaw puzzle, must be put in place before the total picture becomes apparent. Not that any one piece is more important than another but it seems that certain pieces have been hidden for too long, as is the case in this country, with reincarnation.

The continuity of life and reincarnation into this plane called Earth is an accepted fact by over half the world's population. The American Indian is taught this as a child. In the East, it is part of the religious teachings—as it was once part of the teachings of Christianity. All references to reincarnation were stricken from the Holy Scriptures by the Byzantine emperor Justinian (483–565 A.D.), although it would be more correct to say that the whole credo of the Christian Church was edited by and for Empress Theodora during the reign of her husband, Emperor Justinian.*

Asked where in our scriptures reincarnation was definitely taught, Cayce said, "John, 6–8 and 3–5, then the rest as a whole." (452-6) Theodora's rape was apparently not as thorough as she might have wished.

The unveiled truth of the matter was withheld a mere fifteen hundred years, a drop in the ocean of eternal time, but a seeming eternity to those living in ignorance of this understanding.

We might think of our various lives in the earth plane as so many beads in a box, but until we have strung them together to form, as it were, a necklace, it is difficult to see our development—our growth—to an evolved state.

But "It is never too late to mend thy ways. For life is eternal and ye are today what ye are because of what ye have been. For years the co-creator with thy Maker, that ye may one day be present with all those who love His coming." (5284-1)

You are happy today because of the happiness you have given others in previous lifetimes. You are beautiful because of the beauty you have built into your soul's pattern. If you are not as beautiful today as you would like to be, then start building your future NOW. "It is never too late to mend thy ways."

Although we are not dealing primarily with the fact of returning souls, the understanding of this truth is necessary for the comprehension of matters to be dealt with further. These other important facets such as astrology, music and color, dreams and the finer sense perceptions, although complex in themselves, will appear less so once the continuity of life is accepted and appreciated.

Living in a three-dimensional plane, our senses limited to five

* See Noel Langley, ed., *The Hidden History of Reincarnation* (Virginia Beach, Va.: ARE Press, 1965).

(or six) it will take some effort to reach that state of being wherein one can view life as more than a series of connected intervals in time and space and live in the ETERNAL PRESENT and its attendant contentment. "What is time or space when thou art in those influences that make for contentment in thine inner soul? Save those that wander from the knowledge of embracing the moment. For, only one at a time [lives] may be experienced—if they are divided as such. But see and know all rather as one." (541-1)

Q. If the soul is eternal, why is the memory finite?

A. "As man finds himself in the consciousness of a material world materiality has often, in the material-minded, blotted out the consciousness of a soul." (262-89)

The purpose for something was always stressed in the readings. What would be the purpose of knowing about all our lives? It might only confuse us. Cayce opened life readings by stating that all the experiences in the earth would not be indicated but only those which directly affected our present experience.

"For thyself came not merely by chance. For the earth is a causation world; in the earth cause and effect are as the natural law. And as each soul enters this material plane it is to meet or to give those lessons or truths that others, too, may gain the more knowledge of the purpose for which each soul enters." (3645-1)

The developments which our bodies require—the effects of causes set up through many lifetimes—may not always be tackled in one lifetime. The circumstances would not fit all the situations needed to be resolved and the complexity of tangent karma which might arise would involve monumental complications.

Q. "Have I learned the lessons I came here to learn?"

A. "Life and Truth and understanding are a growth. As we

apply the lessons we learn, in our dealings with our fellow man, do we indeed as entities and souls comprehend their full meaning. Hence this experience is as a growth, as an unfoldment even as the lotus that ye adopted as a portion of the service of those in the Temple Beautiful. Unfold, the seeds come after. Seek and ye shall know, knock and it will be opened." (1246-2)

The Temple Beautiful existed in Egypt approximately twelve thousand five hundred years ago. After visiting the Temple of Sacrifice—what might be considered a hospital today—where surgery was performed, using the techniques of the day which were apparently more advanced than our present day techniques, entities would then enter the Temple Beautiful for instruction in meditation, movement, color and sound. They would live there in what we would call a program of total immersion.

Of the Temple of Sacrifice; it was a place where there was the "crucifying of the activities of the body, the desires of the flesh. . . . These must be blotted out as each soul offers itself in sacrifice that it may be put upon the altars or fires of love and *burned*, as it were, that there might be that purification in the flesh that there might become again the dross burned away and the pure soul be one with the Creative Energy." (1246-2)

There were many ways of 'burning' the unwanted activities of a body: "Then there may be seen, the attuning of the music as may be in the day; the viola tuned to the vibrations of the fires of nature may be destructive or smothering or aflaming same." (275-43)

After the purification—after all unwanted parts of a body had been taken care of in whatever manner—however incomprehensible it may be to us at the moment, came the tuning—the fine tuning—in the Temple Beautiful. ". . . in that first school established as a curative and as a preventative . . . and those various conditions that dealt with the developments of the *inner* man." (275-11) "When there became the necessity of establishing the temples where there were the studies of the *combinations of diet*—as in purifying the body from the blood . . . took on such activities as to remove the scourges that arose from certain characters of diets. And there were brought through the feedings more symmetrical and harmonious proportions on the bodies . . ." "those that made music for those as they swayed in body-movement—as in the chants that aided the indwelling raising of the thoughts in the power which impelled through *thinking* [as would be termed today], or the attuning of the spiritual selves to the attunements of the Universal Forces." (275-33) "temples that were for worshipfulness of the peoples to those influences or forces that made them whole in body and mind." (275-40) "Then to thy service in the Temple Beautiful. Here we have those incantations that are as but the glorifying of the constructive forces in all of their activity within the human emotions that may be known in the present day." (275-43)

Cayce looked to the past that he might enlighten us as to our present condition and inspire us to hopefully build for the future.

Homer's *Odyssey* was a short trip compared to the one we are on. But a trip connotes going from one point to another. If we think of our existence as a pleasure cruise, we will come closer to the attitude with which we may enjoy life. When one embarks upon a cruise, returning is the last thing to enter the mind. The thoughts one *does* entertain are those of fellowship, sea air and healthful living, and a recuperating of all forces, knowing that at the journey's end he will be a more healthy, refreshed individual and able to tackle whatever work has to be performed.

Throughout these various 'experiences' in the earth plane we sometimes change our sex to experience a certain development. However, 3379-2 was what might be called 'ultra-feminine' and Cayce gave, as the reason, the following: "For here again we find an entity every whit a woman, not having changed its sex in its experience in the earth, no wonder the entity doesn't understand men, nor men understand the entity. They cannot think in the same channel, not having experienced that which is the prompting urge from a first cause and a twig or a rib out of the first cause, for these are rarely considered in their correct relationships as man to woman."

From this we see the necessity of experiencing all phases of development for our own good. For our understanding.

A reading given in 1944 for 3653-1 is most exciting. Cayce opened by remarking "What an unusual record—and one of those who might be termed as physically the mothers of the world! For the entity was one of those in the ark.

"For the entity has appeared when there were new revelations to be given. And again when it appears there are new revelations to be made.

"May the entity so conduct its mind, its body and its purposes, then, as to be a channel through which such messages may come that are needed for the awakenings in the minds of men as to the necessity for returning to the search for their relationship with Creative Forces, or God."

A reading given for 3514-1 in 1943 gave: "For as has been indicated, now, in the next few years there will be many entrances of those who are to prepare the way for the new race, the new experience of man, that may be a part of these activities in preparation for the day of the Lord."

All those born in this cycle, please take note and don't let yourselves be caught napping.

Just for fun, let us look at some names of famous people who reincarnated in time to get a Cayce reading: Thomas Jefferson; Joan of Arc; Pocahontas; Sir Joshua Reynolds; Frances Willard; Marie Antoinette; Mary Magdalene; and even a couple of the disciples.

This is truly an age in which great things will happen.

CHAPTER *11* *Recycling the Mental Body*

GETTING A NEW CHARGE OUT OF LIFE

is the builder! Mind is the builder! Mind is the builder! Mind is

To understand this statement completely, pause for a moment and consider certain basic truths. This concept will be envisioned in the mind of each according to his development. It ws given in its pure and simple essence through Cayce thus: "The basis, then: Know O Israel (Know O people) the Lord thy God is one!

"From this premise we would reason that: in the manifestation of all power, force, motion, vibration, that which impels, that which detracts, is in its essence of one *force,* one source, in its elemental form." (262-52)

From this we must realize that in *everything* there is this motion or force. "Thus there are the vibrations of the electrical energies of the body, for life itself is electrical . . ." (281-27)

Think of this. If life is a collection of electrical forces, each atom as well as each body has its positive and negative poles. Oriental philosophy has named these Yin and Yang. Indian philosophy acknowledges the Divine Mother as well as the Heavenly Father. "For these vibratory principles as we find my son are the basic elemental principles of truth itself." (707-1)

"In the beginning there was the force of attraction and the force that repelled." (262-52)

This is simple enough. Remember the magnetic dogs? One side was the negative side and the other the positive. If you put two positive ends together, it would push the dog away—the same with two negatives. Yet if you put a positive to a negative, they would click together. "God, the first cause, the first principle, the first movement, IS!" (262-52)

This must be our point of agreement. Let us assume that the earth has a negative charge, or receptive principle. Remember it is sometimes called Mother Earth, and has a Yin quality. Let us assume that the 'force' which is the first cause, is a positive charge, or directive principle. This is our Heavenly Father and has a Yang quality.

A person, being both of the earth and of God, can exhibit either the positive or the negative principle, the Yang or the Yin, depending upon the state of consciousness with which one is in tune. "When this first cause comes into man's experience in the present realm [Earth] he becomes confused, in that he appears to have an influence upon this force or power in directing same. Certainly! Much, though, in the manner as the reflection of light in a mirror." (262-52)

Bearing in mind the illustration of the dogs—if we use this force, much as reflecting it off a mirror, we are acting as a positive charge and deflecting this force from us and directing it outwards.

Science has proven that every atom contains a positive and a negative charge and Cayce tells us, "Hence in man's consciousness he becomes aware of what is known as the atomic or cellular form of movement." We must now disperse what we formerly thought of as mind being located in the brain—and think of it rather as an electrical impulse being sent from the brain (headquarters, as it were) to each and every cell of the body. It is now possible to understand the statement that "each as an entity is a miniature copy of the universe, possessing a physical body, a mental body and a spiritual body." (262-10)

As the will is directive (as opposed to receptive), we must attribute a positive charge to the will. For, "Know, no urge surpasses the individual will of an entity, that birthright of each soul, that gift of the Creative Forces that makes or causes the *individuality* in an entity, the ability to know itself to be itself and yet one with the Creative Forces." (2629–1)

In exerting our will, we are using a positive charge—which attracts us to the negative charge of the earth, and, incidentally keeps us there. But by becoming receptive, exercising our negative charge, we are releasing ourselves from the ties which bind us to the earth and thus no longer repelling the Creative Forces.

At cellular level, we are a physical body. At the same time we are a spiritual body—each atom of our body being charged with the energy from the first cause or spirit. The mind determines the electrical patterns which are exhibited. When we think about it, everything is electrical—or vibrating. Imagine the sounds of the day coming into our bodies as vibrations and then being transformed by the brain into electrical patterns and circulated through our systems and digested by each and every cell. Similarly, with whatever we may see, smell and touch. We are building a computer-like bank of memories into each and every cell. We might now call these memories the subconscious, for, "the subconscious mind is both consciousness and thought or spirit consciousness. Hence may be classified, in the physical sense, as a habit." (262–10)

Now we see that we are reacting to what we have fed into our systems—our mental body—in the form of habits.

These reactions to daily circumstances, to life, can be continued as habits ad infinitum—or they can, with our new knowledge, be charged in reverse and change the patterns into more constructive ones. "Though there may be disturbing influences, these may be overcome through the practicing of just the opposite." (1580–1)

The motto of the school of method acting is "Act—don't react." Might we not take this motto for our own as we face the variety of situations which can now be overcome because of our new awareness?

If we continue using the same old cells all the time—they will tire with overuse and the ones not being used will atrophy. This imbalance brings illness, disease.

Be awake. Don't live in a semiconscious state, allowing habit patterns from the subconscious to determine the way you face a situation. If we automatically (as habit) react to life as we have reacted in the past, we are caught in the wheel of karma, or memory, until we have learned to act according to our higher self—or higher knowledge. A memory must be recognized as a stepping stone on the path if it is to play a helpful part in our development.

The first step is "being able, as it were, to *literally* stand aside and watch self go by!" (262-9)

We must *consciously* act as we *want* to act. "Apply that we know" as Cayce would say, and monitor what goes into the memory bank for "as indicated as a part of a body-consciousness, that which a mind and a body entertains or applies becomes a part of that individual entity, shining forth in its relationships to men as a personality and shortly in that superconsciousness as individuality. That bears its relationship to the Creative Forces." (2174-2)

Envision some of the situations with which you are faced daily. Is your reaction always the same—or at least predictable enough to follow a pattern? When you are confronted by an irate acquaintance, or a hostile stranger, do your feathers get ruffled? Ask yourself—and answer yourself truly—if somebody were to strike you, would you instinctively strike back? If you answered yes to these questions, even once, you have memory patterns which need re-programming if you are to become a serene and poised beauty.

In the modern world, it is difficult to pass a day without encountering at least one person or situation with equilibrium less than perfect. Do not face the situation as a problem to be overcome—why not consider it an opportunity for soul development? So when this opportunity arises, "remember, no man is bigger than that which makes him lose his temper." (254-55)

There is no more sorry sight than that of a woman 'blowing her cool' as is termed by the young people of today. As there is a graceful way to sit, to get into and out of a car, there is also a graceful way to use (not lose) one's temper, when the situation calls for it. But for the sake of health, 2-14 was told: "Aggravation of mental forces and a distraughtness often come, producing headaches, nervousness and a continual reaction throughout the hypogastric system. This causes nausea and an over-production of hydrochloric acid in the stomach itself. *Such reactions should be a warning to every human being.* ANGER IS A CERTAIN POISON TO THE SYSTEM. Anger can destroy the brain as well as any disease, for it is itself a disease of the mind." (3510-1)

Much has been spoken of a mother carrying a child affecting the child within. Even during the period of nursing, great care must be taken by the mother not to transmit negative influences to the child. Case 1208-2 had a five-day-old baby and asked Cayce if there were any special foods to be avoided by the mother. She must have had a fiery temper for Cayce's answer was that "*fats* are the most detrimental to *all* infants in this developing stage." Then he added "and ANGER! Keep from ANGER!"

This does not mean that one should just go through life as a punching bag or a doormat. Turning the other cheek is well and good unless there are principles at stake which must be defended. Whenever the subject of righteous anger arises, it brings to mind the story of Jesus in the temple overturning the tables of the moneychangers. "Righteous anger is a virtue. He who has not temper is very weak; but he who controls not his temper is much worse." (3416-1)

What does that word righteous mean? It is given to us so often as an attribute that should be instilled into our very being. "What is righteousness? Just being kind, just being noble, just being self sacrificing, just being willing to be the hands for the blind, the feet for the lame." (5753-2)

How then should one act instead of reacting to these disturbing influences? "These very influences *spiritualized* may make for soul development, even though it passes through hardships, that will bring peace, happiness, joy and harmony. Are not these the opposite of hate, malice, and contention?" (476-1)

We must at all costs avoid going against universal laws—rather attune ourselves to them. The fear of the Lord is the beginning of wisdom. The fear to face life is the beginning of disharmony. Not because it distorts the features of a pretty face, or causes wrinkles, but because "fear brings that of contempt first from those that *bring* same, and then the seed is the dissatisfaction in self, and condemnation of self's position." (2686-1)

Those who are in the business world, and must answer to an employer, should think carefully about this trait. "Never, never be afraid." (1981-1) for "fear creates doubt." (2272-1) and "because ye doubt others, know it is because others cannot trust you! If ye doubt in this way or that way, or manner, look into thy own purposes!" (1668-1)

Self-confidence and poise are essential if one is to succeed in the business world. This confidence can only come with the knowledge that there is a definite purpose for you being wherever you are at the moment. If you are honestly fulfilling a need for your fellowman and performing your task, whatever it is, to the best of your ability, you cannot be other than confident. We are told that like begets like. In the physical, opposite electromagnetic currents attract. In the higher vibrational world of spirit, the reverse holds true. These electrical patterns of our thoughts are, when activated, attractive to the same thoughts in others. They are contagious, as it were. So if we have doubts about ourselves, it follows that others will have doubts about us.

This same rule applies when the 'girls' get together over coffee. Should their subject of conversion be an absent party, they should practice charity. Sacha Guitry—the French wit—once said that two women always ended up agreeing with each other over the back of a third. But these two women are merely joining forces for their own destruction. When one finds fault with another, it is usually to bolster oneself. Case 3376-1 was given the injunction: "To get a better surety in self as to its spiritual outlook, leave off the finding of faults, and so many faults will not be found with you. Leave off speaking unkindly. If it is impossible to say nice things about a person, keep silent—even though what you say may be true. Remember, there's so much good in the worst of us that it doesn't behoove the best of us to speak unkindly of any of the rest of us."

To say good all the time is not easy. Some might fear appearing too much like a Pollyanna. "The peculiarities, the oddities, the errors are to be minimized, NOT dwelt upon and increased! Minimize rather than crystalize or magnify any faults in the other." (1722-1)

Minimize the faults and magnify the virtues. That is a workable rule. It does not say eliminate the faults, nor see only virtues, it simply tells you to adjust the balance of the two. "Be not faultfinding ever, for when ye find fault, ye may be sure others will find fault with thee. Let peace, then, and mercy guide thy words, and thy activities, day by day." (262-116)

So many things can hurt us. Holding a grudge against a person or situation is for some far easier than letting the situation go. Resentments build up in our being and can reside in us indefinitely. As Alexander Pope said: "To err is human, to forgive divine." It is simple to say "O.K. I forgive . . . but I'll never forget." This attitude will be to our own disadvantage. "For to hold grudges, to hold malice, to hold those things that create or bring contention, only builds the barrier to prevent thy OWN inner self enjoying peace and contentment." (1608-1)

Not only does the holding of resentments and grudges prevent inner peace in the spiritual—for remember that body, mind and spirit are all one—consider what it does in the physical. "Resentments . . . naturally create within the system those secretions that are hard upon any circulation, and especially where there is disturbance with the spleen, the pancreas and a portion of the liver." (470-19)

"An attitude of *resentment* will produce inflammation. An attitude of any internal activity, or holding that desire as needed will assist in the psychopathic effect had upon the nerves of the system, and especially through the ileum-plexus. Know what is to be done, then just consciously watch it act! There is not inflammation in the appendix. There is in the caecum, where this impaction occurs." (1005-7)

At the entrance to the colon is the ileo-caecal valve; to create an impaction in that area sets up all sorts of possibilities for physical ills. If resentments are the Pandora's box of the mind, surely the colon is their physical counterpart.

How can we overcome resentments? It is easy enough for one to say "don't hold grudges," but how is one supposed to sweep these thoughts away? Removing something without replacing it with something else creates a void. Let us concentrate, not so much on throwing away what we *don't* want, but on displacing it by taking on the qualities which we *do* want.

One helpful solution to the overcoming of resentments is "the manner in which ye treat others, ye are treating thy Maker. Keep this much in mind and resentments will not be so much a part of thy conclusions. It is not thyself by nature but conclusions." (2982-1)

Worry, worry, worry. It must be a part of the American make-up or the sad-faced worry bird made of a pine cone which is sold in novelty shops all over the country would never have been the success that it was. Worry is the direct opposite of contentment and we will remember that contentment comes with living in the moment. "In whatsoever state one finds oneself, make self content; not satisfied, but content." (137-7)

We are in the present. Dwelling in the past brings frustrations and living in the future causes anxieties—so why can't we just learn to 'be'? We are beings—albeit human. Our spirit however is made in the image of our Maker and is eternal, so what is the rush? "Do not burden self with that as is unnecessary to be met until the time arises, for worry killeth." (900-345)

When one's mind is burdened, one either sits and worries—or seeks escape. The varieties of methods of escape are manifold. Sometimes one retires to bed to regroup one's forces, but 1236-1 was told that "the body gets sufficient rest, if it didn't worry! Worry is harder on the body than lack of rest. . . ." "See and know that worry will only unfit and prevent the body from meting out the best in self and for others." (39-4)

What, then, is the formula for counteracting worry? "Keep an even mental balance. DON'T WORRY!"

Cayce, recognizing immediately that he might have set up a

complex electrical thought pattern, *i.e.* worrying about worrying, gave 646-1 a modus operandi to combat this. "It is easy to say 'Don't worry,' but how may a person prevent it? By keeping control of the mind, not only through the very will of self but by keeping occupied in doing something for others."

What are the physical symptoms of worry? Case 1523-5 inquired about the cause of the circles under her eyes and was told that they came from a "nervous condition, and WORRY."

Through the thousands of readings about health, past lives and a general philosophy of existence emerged patterns for living. One law which surfaced at regular intervals was that sickness is caused by sin. And when questioned about sin, Cayce said that all man's sin could be traced back to the 'self'. When man exerts his will he becomes more of the earth, enmeshed in its influences. But when man relinquishes this will—as he does in sleep—his forces recuperate and his body is recharged with divine power. This is one of the principles of meditation.

Many times we can recognize the sin as being selfish, but there are other times when this is not so obvious. Humility is one of the virtues to be sought, but even some seek virtue for self-gratification, not realizing that virtue is its own reward.

Case 1315-2 was told that "the entity often . . . rather belittles self's abilities. Humbleness is well; but 'who lighteth the candle and putteth it under a bushel?'

"For while selflessness is the law, to belittle self is a form of selfishness and not selfless." (2803-2)

A perfect example of such false humility was Dickens' character, Uriah Heep, who hid behind his obsequiousness as a bandit hides behind a mask. He would not—could not—be himself, so he became something far worse. He is certainly one whom none of us wishes to emulate.

Poise is sought by every woman. It is the featured promise on every charm school brochure. However, it cannot be acquired by walking around the room with a book balanced on your head. When asked how to acquire poise and overcome timidity, Cayce answered, "Be YOURSELF." (2936-2)

To be yourself, you must know yourself, and you can't do

this either by walking around with a book on your head. Only after we discover the little traits and habits which make up the self can we relinquish them and start on the road to selflessness. "Then, self must become selfless, and not in any form or manner desire those things that would be advantageous over others in that others would have to suffer that self might have the advantage—for that is selfishness, and not selflessness.

"And selflessness is that which each entity, each soul, must attain through the varied experiences in the material plane." (2185-1)

Patience, according to Cayce, is one dimension of our three-dimensional world, the other two being time and space. Only in the world as we know it do these exist—for if there was no time, and no space, who would need patience? "Time and space and patience, then, are those channels through which man as a finite mind may become aware of the infinite.

For each phase of time, each phase of space, is dependent as one atom upon another. And there is no vacuum, for this, as may be indicated in the universe, is an impossibility with God. Then there is no time, there is no space, when patience becomes manifested in love." (3161-1)

Does this give a new meaning to "in patience possess ye your souls"?

We must learn these laws of the universe, for without them we risk facing these daily situations with annoyance indefinitely until we can understand them and accept them for what they are: opportunities. "There comes the indication that the entity is meeting problems which have been problems before. *What* causes, what produces problems in the experience of an entity—either in its mental or material self? That of non-compliance to the laws, the purposes for which Creative Forces have given the opportunities to the individual entity." (2427-1)

When we have faced these "opportunities" we can relax in our much-prized contentment. But "the greater an individual, the more content an individual may be. Not as an animal that is satisfied with the body filled, but rather that contentment that is seen in the acts of those that bring joy with the expression of themselves; as a bird in song, a bird in flight, an animal in the care of its young. *That* is contentment; the other rather lethargy." (347-2)

One of the major laws of the universe and one which can work for weal or woe is the law of expectancy. For without it, there is no goal. A beautiful example of this law in action was displayed when 3564-1 asked if there was likelihood of bad health in March? Cayce told her: "If you are looking for it you can have it in February! If you want to skip March, skip it—you'll have it in June! If you want to skip June, don't have it at all this year."

This truly makes one stop and think about his expectations. Do you stock up with aspirin and extra oranges and tea bags when you hear that a flu epidemic is raging? When asked if you have had a cold this year, do you answer "not yet"? The big secret is not in the expecting alone, but in the expecting and BELIEVING. "Each individual is, in reality, that manifestation of the individual's conception of the impelling force from within, whether it be termed or called God, Nature, Universal Forces, natural powers or what not." (900-234)

We are living and projecting what our conception of God is. "If an individual doesn't expect great things of God, he has a very poor God, hasn't he?" (462-10)

How often do we hear someone say "I hate Pittsburgh . . ." or "I hate opera . . ." Maybe for some it is a misguided interpretation of sophistication—the affectation of jaded tastes. This attitude arouses anything but admiration if truth were known. Hate is a destructive force and one to be avoided. If a food is not pleasing, avoid it—do not hate it. If a place is incompatible —do not go there. Expressing one's preference for something else should never be done through an expression of hate.

Cayce taught us: "Do not belittle, do not hate, for hate creates and brings turmoil and strifes.

"As to the associations with others, if ye would have friends, show thyself friendly. This does not mean becoming the butt of other's fun, nor of thy using others in the same manner. But if ye would have love, love others." (1537–1)

Love is something which we all seek. It is the answer to everything. Love makes the world go round, literally. What is law? Love. What is love? God. What is God? Love and law.

Judging from the many computerized dating services and advertised lonely hearts clubs throughout the country, many people are seeking love. If the astronomical number of divorces can be relied upon to tell a tale, it seems that finding a mate is not always a guarantee of finding love.

Case 1786–2 was asked: "Is there really the desire to know love, or to know the experience of someone having an emotion over self? Is it a desire to be itself expended in doing that which may be helpful or constructive? This CAN be done, but it will require the LOSING of self . . . IN service for others. . . .

"But arise to that consciousness that if ye would have life, if ye would have friends, if ye would have love, these things ye must expend. For only that ye give away do ye possess."

Why do marriages go on the rocks? Why do they fail? Many have a misguided conception of marriage—thinking that once the knot is tied, both parties can relax and let the other do the work. 838–1 was told: "Remember each, love is giving; it is a growth. It may be cultivated or it may be seared. That of selflessness on the part of each is necessary. Remember, the union of body, mind and spirit in such as marriage should ever be not for the desire of self but as *one*. Love grows; love endures; love forgiveth; love understands; love keeps those things rather as opportunities that to others would become hardships.

"Then, do not sit *still* and expect the other to do all the giving, nor all the forgiving; but make it rather as the unison and the purpose of each to be that which is a complement one to the other ever." "O that all would learn that love is all embracing and NOT merely possession!" (1816-1)

Too many people mistake a marriage contract for a certificate of ownership. How often have you heard a woman introducing her mate with the emphasis on the possessive pronoun "MY" husband. "Let love be without dissimulation—that is without POSSESSION, but as in that manner as He gave, 'Love one another, even as I have loved you;' willing to give the life, the self, for the purpose, for an ideal. Other than this, these become as that which will bring in the experience that in which each will hate self and blame the other." (413-11) "Love in its greatest aspect, does not possess! It IS. It is not then possessive to be real." (1821-1)

Now that we have possibly clarified what love is not, "seek to know indeed what LOVE is. For there is a star of hope only in those who seek to manifest love, whether of a spiritual, mental or even material import. In such there is hope—and without it, little hope, or little stability." (1946-1) "Become then a channel of blessings to others, and thus may the beauties of the heavenly forces—as may be expressed in such—be thine very own. Beauty for beauty's sake. Love that it may be the manifestation of not bodily emotions but rather those that show forth His activity in and among men." (1189-1)

Now is the time to relinquish those old thought patterns which have limited you in the past. In the Cayce wisdom there are indeed new lamps for old and each one has a genie all its own.

The mind is the blueprint for the whole structure of our being. Make sure you have a plan which can be relied upon; what is your ideal? Can you construct from your blueprint as it now stands a worthy edifice—or would it be a hovel? Realizing your part in the whole scheme of things and your true worth, don't settle for less than a palace—you deserve it. It is your legacy.

> "KEEP THE HEART SINGING!
> KEEP THE MIND CLEAR!
> KEEP THE FACE TOWARD THE LIGHT!
> THE SHADOWS THEN ARE BEHIND."
>
> (39-4)

CHAPTER *12* *Vibratory Influences*

ASTROLOGICAL SOJOURNS, GEMS AND STONES,
SCENTS, MUSIC AND COLOR

WHETHER WE like it or not, we are influenced in our daily activities by vibrations of which we may be unconscious—circumstances beyond our control.

The myriad psychological tactics employed by Madison Avenue and the media are to most of us so transparent by now that they are not worth considering, nor are the various sales techniques which are exercised upon a presumably unsuspecting public.

This section will deal rather with influences which might have hitherto been unrecognized *as influences*. Colors, for example, have always had their effect upon us, but only recently are we becoming aware that certain colors are deeply involved in our state of well-being. Though music hath charms to soothe the savage beast, it also soothes the higher aspects of man as well. In the last twenty years piped music has been installed just about everywhere, in offices and factories, elevators, waiting rooms and even washrooms. It has sometimes been called canned euphoria —but the influence of music is recognized to have a positive effect upon people.

We have all heard that diamonds are a girl's best friend, but many would be surprised to learn that lapis lazuli emanates certain vibrations that give strength and self assurance to one wearing it.

Some of these influences can be put to work for us, so why should we, through ignorance of their potential, allow these influences to go to waste or even work against us?

3659-1 was urged: "Do learn music. It partakes of the beauty of the spirit. For remember, music alone may span that space between the finite and the infinite. In the harmony of sound, the harmony of color, even the harmony of motion itself, beauty is all akin in the expression of the soul self, in the harmony of the mind, to be properly used in relationship to the body . . . let much of thy life be controlled by the same harmony that is in the best music, yea and even in the worst, for it too, has its place."

There are some plants who might not agree with Cayce, however. In 1971, tests were made exposing two sets of control plants to music. One set was graced with music by Debussy, the other exposed to 'acid rock.' The former flourished, while the other started first growing away from the source of the music and gradually died. There is music, and there is music: "And there is music of the spheres, there is music of the growing things of nature. There is music of the growing of the rose, of *every* plant that bears color, of every one that opens its blossoms for the edification of the environs." (949–12) . . . and there is music. "For music is of the soul, and yet one may become mind and soul sick for certain kinds of music, or soul and mind sick from certain kinds of music." (5401–1)

The awareness that music and color are closely interwoven is becoming more apparent in our own experience. Case 2779–1 inquired from the playing of which instrument would the most satisfaction be received. "The violin here. The entity gets *color* rather than what is already called the tonal vibration . . . though the tonal vibration is that which PRODUCES color . . . color and tone are just different rates of vibration."

"Many a soul may find God in a song and never in a flower—

yet in both are color and tone and natural influences." (5398–1)

Case 5122–1 was told that "music and flowers, then, should be the entity's work through this experience. . . . Flowers will love the entity, as the entity loves flowers. Very few flowers would wither while about or on this body. . . .

"Consider the color, the beauty of the lily as it grows from its ugly muck, or the shrinking violet as it sends out its color, its odor to enrich even the very heart of God.

"Consider the rose and how it unfolds with the color of the day, opening itself to the sunshine and the rain. . . .

"For flowers should be the companionship of those who are lonely. For they may speak to the 'shut-in.' They may bring color again to the cheeks of those who are ill. They may bring to the bride the hope of love, of beauty, of a home. For flowers love the places where there is peace and rest. Sunshine and shadows, yes. There are varieties from those of the open fields to those which grow in the bog—but they grow.

"Why won't people learn the lesson from them and grow, in love and in beauty, in whatever may be their environ?" "For as has been given, color is but vibration. Vibration is movement. Movement is activity of a positive and negative force. Is the activity of self as in relationship to these then positive?" (281–29)

Case 967–3 had been working on a method to solve the complex matter of color harmony, and wanted to know how to advance the cause of greater harmony in this realm. The answer: "Color is vibration, like overtones in music. These ye have applied occasionally. Then use them in attuning thy body consciousness to those vibrations about thee, which may—in some instances—take on color also. Use not for self alone, but using, do not abuse."

Through the readings emerged an understanding of the endocrine system as it relates to the universe. The glands were referred to as contacts between the physical and spiritual bodies. Their vibrations can be discerned through color. "As is known, vibration is the essence or the basis of color. As color and vibration then become to the consciousness along the various centers in an individual's experience in meditation made aware, they come to mean definite experiences. Just as anger is red, or as something depressing is blue; yet in their shades, their tones, their activities, to each they begin with the use of same in the experience to mean those various stages.

"For instance, while red is anger, rosy to most souls means delight and joy—yet to others, as they are formed in their transmission from center to center—come to mean or to express what manner of joy; whether that as would arise from a material, a mental or a spiritual experience. Just as may be seen in the common interpretation of white but with all manner of rays from same begins or comes to mean that above the aura of all in its vibrations from the body and from the activity of the mental experience when the centers are vibrating to color." (281-30)

3637-1 was told that "these would indicate that the entity through its mental self has passed through all the urges from the vibrations of that ordinarily called color. For color itself is vibration, just as much vibration as—or even more than—music. These might be indicated then, as the various colors and the notes of music on each. . . . By the colors indicated ye can control thine own physical being, by thine own hand."

Edgar Cayce, fully awake, could see auras: that is, colors or a colored energy field emanating from an individual. This is a phenomenon shared by many sensitives, or psychics. For years Cayce thought that everyone saw these colors until he mentioned it and realized that it was a very special gift. Not all of us see auras—but so many of us sense them in one way or another. We pick up the vibrations from the people we contact. It is possible that this sensing might have to do with the aura for 275-31. She asked for the meaning of her aura—which was blue and purple. "As the color or tone indicates—the blue in purity and the purple towards spirituality." She then asked the best colors to wear and was told, "Blue and those tones or shades that go toward the deep or royal purple, and the modes that are in between." Asked what colors should surround her: "Those of the

gold and blue are healing colors, as is purple for the body."
There seems to be a direct relationship to the colors recommended and the auric colors. "Thus we find that dress, certain
colors and tones have much of a 'feel' in the experience of the
entity. And if the entity will wear white, mauve and shades of
purple, it will ever be as helpful vibrations to the entity. For
what is builded from any experience in the earth is as a habit
in the present, having that same character of influence upon an
individual's ability toward those things and conditions; not having power within themselves, but as that which has been builded
by the entity." (3395-2)

Case 288-38 asked what were her best colors, and then asked
"Or does it really make any difference?" "Each body, each activity, each soul entity vibrates better to this, that or the other
color. As with this, certain colors of green and blue are those
to which the body vibrates better."

She then asked if we are supposed to spiritualize colors? "Colors
are the natural spiritualizations of tone and sound; they are
naturally spiritualizations of same."

"Hence the red, the deep coral, upon thine flesh will bring
quietness in those turmoils that have arisen within the inner
self; as also will the pigments of blue to the body bring the
air, the fragrance of love, mercy, truth and justice that is within
self." (694-2) "You will rarely find individuals being intolerant
with others with something intrinsically carved being worn—
or never very, very mad with blue being worn." (578-2) "Those
of purple and of gold present the highest of that obtained in
color vibration." (2087-3)

The use of color and music in healing is being re-discovered;
its true worth is increasingly appreciated. "Sounds, music and
colors may have much to do with creating the proper vibrations
about individuals that are mentally unbalanced, physically
deficient or ill in body and mind; and may be used as helpful
experiences." (1334-1)

The use of music in hospitals is becoming more apparent—but
there is still room for growth. Also, music is being used in

mental hospitals as part of occupational therapy programs. It is the ideal way to bring harmony into the vibrations of a disturbed patient. Playing favorite tunes requested by patients not only brings harmony into their patterns of behavior, but also brings them into the activities of a group. And until we learn that others are more important than ourselves, we are all in need of some help.

Music is used extensively in teaching the mentally retarded, starting first with rhythm. The child is given a percussive instrument and encouraged to play along with the piano or phonograph. The rhythm that is kept by the child is an indication of its coordination and the progress it will make.

Asked what course of study should be pursued in secondary and higher education, Cayce said: "Music! The history and activity of music in various forms. If you learn music, you'll learn history. If you learn music, you'll learn mathematics. If you learn music, you'll learn all there is to learn—unless it's something bad." (3053-3)

Music appreciation should be a part of all training—whether in hospitals, schools or as extra-curricular activity after school. Music is one of the free gifts of life. The ability to enjoy it lies within ourselves, and often a simple course of music appreciation can open this door into a wonderland of moods, color and sound which has the power to replenish lost energy, soothe frayed nerves and reintroduce harmony after it has been allowed to drift.

With new instruments being developed all the time, our sense of hearing is becoming more and more acute. We are conscious on more levels now than ever before. But there are still sound vibrations to which we are not given access, for example the high pitch of a dog whistle which the dog hears and which we cannot.

Color is also a perception or an awareness which is still in the process of evolving, which might explain its recent use in so-called psychedelic art. Dissection of the eyes of apes and monkeys shows that all parts necessary for the perception of

color are present and could be used; however, they are not.
Color tests with children show that red is the first color to draw
their attention, while blue is the last. Primitive art employed as
its colors red, yellow and black.

In his book *Pain, Sex and Time,* Gerald Heard points out
that the words used to describe colors were quite rudimentary
until comparatively lately.* In Homer's Greece there were half
a dozen words denoting the color red but none for blue and
green. The Greeks in those days could pick out the red in the
purple of the Mediterranean but were blind to the blue. This
would explain Homer's constant reference to the "wine-dark
sea."

However refined our senses may be, we cannot fail to see
how limited they are. As long as there are auras waiting to be
seen, the sounds of roses growing to be heard and odors that
will give flight to our souls awaiting acknowledgment, evolve-
ment is possible.

3008–1 was told "during those rest periods after the fume
bath and massage, do rest for at least fifteen minutes under
the ultra-violet light, but do have always the green light pro-
jected between the ultra-violet and the body. The ultra-violet
should be at least sixty inches from the body, and only the
mercury light. The green light should be 8 by 10 inches or 10
by 12 inches [dimensions of the green glass covering same] and
about 14 to 18 inches from the body. These are healing influences of that taken out of the infra-ray, see?" "Colors will also
find an influence in the entity's activities, especially those of not
too severe, but the violet, ultra-violet, shades of green, of mauve,
and pink; though the others may make for a rigor oft in the
entity, the delicate shades—or those as may be termed the spiritual—will influence the entity. When illness or the like were
to come about, soft music and the lighter shades or tones will
quiet where medicine would fail." (773–1)

---

* Gerald Heard, *Pain, Sex and Time: A New Hypothesis of Evolution* (London: Cassell & Co., Ltd., 1939).

Q. Give a color this body might meditate upon beneficially for self healing.

A. "The white light of the Christ if the body itself would find help. It isn't the color, it isn't the vibration. It is rather the awareness of entering into the spirit of truth, the power of love." (1861-11)

It seems that every cosmetic house has at least one special fragrance. Each couture house develops a fragrance which they hope will always be associated with its name. It is interesting to note that about eighty percent of the annual business in the world of fragrance is done during the Christmas season. In the industry, the compounders of perfumes are known as 'noses.' They can usually analyze a fragrance and its ingredients just by smell, so highly refined is their sense of smell. They pick out the top notes first and then the other harmonies and the bass note (or fixative). Case 274 was apparently just such a 'nose.' His readings (7 and 10) dealt with fragrance in great depth. Here are some excerpts: "There is no greater influence in a physical body [and this means animal or man; and man, presumptuously at times, is the higher order of same] than the effects of odors upon the olfactory nerves of the body. . . ."

"For odor is gas and not of the denser matter that makes for such activity in individuals' lives for degrading things. . . ."

"What did Jeroboam that he made the children of Israel sin, but to offer rather the sandalwood of . . . the Egyptians that made for the arousing of the passions in man for the gratifications or the satisfying of his own indulgence. . . ."

"What bringeth the varied odors into the experience of man. Did lavender ever make for bodily associations? Rather has it ever been that upon which the angels of light and mercy would bear the souls of men to a place of mercy and peace."

When starting the reading for 1551-1, Cayce sniffed and said: "You know, it would be very well for the body to change the odors about the room from almonds to lavender and it would be much better."

Another distant observation was made about 1799-1: "Peculiar

—the odor of orris root is about the entity oft, and should be kept close; as the iris as well as a white flower of some kind always." "For the color purple should be close to the body; and the perfumes or odors as of lavender have their influence—not as in great quantity, but that which makes for attunements." (688-2) "Flowers—no matter whether they be in or out of season—are well to be oft about the body. The beauty, the aroma, the aliveness of same will make for vibrations that are most helpful, most beneficial.

"The body becomes quite sensitive to odors, as well as colors; and especially the colors of purple and coral—should be about the body—and rose." (1877-1) "Violet and violet scent with orris are the odors for the entity." (1489-1) "Also the odors which would make for the raising of the vibrations would be lavender or orris root." (379-3) "Odors—have the Life Everlasting about thee often, and ye will find whether as a sachet or as a liquid—it will bring strengthening vibrations to the body." (3416-1)

There have been cases when odors have evoked memories that were hidden deep within the memory cells of an individual; such was the case for 504-3. "Colors and odors have a peculiar effect upon the entity. And when there are the lotus and the sandalwood with cedar they become almost, even yet to the inner senses, overpowering."

The suggestions to wear certain gems about the body appeared in the readings with sufficient regularity to include them as a definite influence. The choice of the gem, however, was such a personal matter, that one can only get clues, then experiment to find the best one for a particular body. But the following excerpts will help in that choice.

Case 440-3, who cut and set stones, was told that "these . . . are not channels to be relied upon except in creating atmosphere. The same thing may be done with an oak tree, or with a persimmon tree—but the activities that come about are because of the emanations thrown off from the stones themselves to the active forces in the body itself."

The idea that a stone gives off emanations which become active with the active forces in a body is a concept that not too many have thought about. One usually chooses jewelry for its appearance as a thing of beauty or a status symbol. Once you have discovered, through careful study and observation, your particular vibrational needs—your choice of a stone will take on a deeper meaning.

Case 531-3 was advised to wear a ruby because "the light or reflection from same worn on hand or body, will enable the body to concentrate in its mental application—through the influences such a stone brings to material expression.

"How? Each element, each stone, each variation of stone, has its own atomic movement, held together by the units of energy which in the universe are concentrated in that particular activity. Hence they come under the varied activities according to their color, vibration, or emanation."

Do you lack self-assurance? The lapis lazuli's color and emanations could rectify that. Its strength is apparently greater than some people can support. More often than not it was recommended that this stone be worn between sheets of glass or encased in crystal, otherwise the emanations would interfere with the cellular activity where it touched the body. Cayce's recommendation for 1981-1 was that this stone should be encased in crystal, but read on for yourself: "As to stones—have near to self, wear preferably upon the body, about the neck, the Lapis Lazuli; this preferably encased in crystal. It will be not merely as an ornament but as strength from the emanation which will be gained by the body always from same. For the stone is itself an emanation of vibrations of the elements that give vitality, virility, strength, and that of assurance in self."

Q. "What precious stone sends out the most healing vibrations for my body?"

A. "Those of the pearl and the bloodstone." (275-31)

The pearl was suggested a few times for its healing vibrations. According to her reading, 951-4 would have been a delight to know. For her, Cayce said that the wearing of the pearl would be not only for the healing but for the creative vibrations and then seemed to intimate that she might use it as a constant reminder that out of irritation emerges a thing of beauty. "All that is beautiful of any nature is of interest to the entity—whether it be a movement of an object, an animal, or the shades and shadows of any phenomena of the atmosphere; a painting, a song. All of these have a resounding vibration in the experience of the entity. . . .

"The pearl should be worn upon the body, or against the flesh of the body; for its vibrations are healing as well as creative— because of the very irritation as produced same, as a defense in the mollusk that produced same. . . .

"Oft the entity has entered or manifested; and thus the body physical and mental is emotional in many directions; as may be indicated from its appreciation of beauty in all its forms— whether the colors in the rainbow, or in the aurora borealis, or in the power and might of a locomotive, or the movement of a swan upon the water, or the denizens of the deep, or the lake or the forest, or whether the movements of the serpent upon the rock, or the eagle in the air, or the fleetness of the hart. All of these, as indicated from the many sojourns, have a definite motivating influence. . . .

"Let these be stepping-stones and not stumbling blocks in thy pursuit of the awareness as to the relationship ye bear to it all."

Case 440-11 was told that: "Listening to the singing of the Lapis Linguis is very similar to listening to a growing tree for days."

Q. "Do trees influence the writing mood?"

A. "They do, in the experience of the entity as well as most individuals." (954-4)

When the Sun squares Uranus and the Moon is in Gemini in the ninth house . . .

The most consulted influence today—by far—is astrology. Did the Delphic oracle ever enjoy such popularity? It seems that the planet Earth after many thousands of years has rediscovered the strength and influence of its fellow planets . . . and new energy has enlivened our vocabulary. A few years ago a 'square' was someone who was not with the times, whereas today the term refers to a difficult aspect in one's natal chart. Making a new contact these days, one is more likely to be asked to give his rising sign than his line of business. Instead of being asked, are you married or single, one is often asked, "Where is your Venus?" Popular musical artists often include their sun signs as part of the vital statistics on their album covers.

How valid is all this? According to Cayce: "The destiny of man lies within the sphere and scope of the planets. That each and every entity passes through the sphere or scope or plane, of each planet, and each existence must have its relation to such an entity."

Q. "Explain how, why and in what manner, planets influence an individual at birth."

A. "As the entity is born into the earth's plane, the relation to that planet, or that sphere, from which the spirit entity took its flight, or its position to enter the earth plane has the greater influence in the earth's plane. Just as the life lived in the earth plane directs to what position the spirit entity takes in the sphere [of earth]." (900-24)

It seems that the planet which we leave upon entering has the greater influence upon us while here. But that the life we live here decides upon our next state of consciousness.

Q. "Does the soul choose the planet to which it goes after each incarnation? If not, what force does?"

A. "In the creation we find all forces relative one with the other, and in the earth's plane that of the flesh. In the develop-

ing from plane to plane becomes the ramification, or the condition of the will merited in its existence finding itself through
aeons of time." (900–10)

If this is difficult to grasp, it might be consolation to know
that scholars who have studied the concept through the readings
still are puzzled by certain aspects. Each year, as their consciousness changes, their personal interpretation of the concept changes.
Maybe this explains why: "Know ye, no one finite mind may
have all the truth." (282–4)

The interim periods between earth lives—which Cayce referred to as astrological sojourns—are as important as the earth
lives. They are the teaching periods for the earth life which
is the proving, the manifesting of all we have learned. "Persona, that radiation through the individual in the earth plane
as received by its development through the spiritual planes, as
we would have in this: we find two entities in an earth plane of
same environment, of same hereditary conditions. One with a
personality, or persona, radiating from every thought or action.
The other submerging every persona it may contact. Different
degrees of development. Persona comes from development then,
either in earth plane or spiritual plane. The persona is acquired
physically, the persona is a natural development. This condition
we find comes nearer to the radiation in astrological condition,
for it partakes of the environment of spheres or universal action
in the developing entity. Hence we find persons born under certain solar conditions have that conditions of persona that radiates in the same direction, while the individual conditions, as
brought to, or given off from such persona, may be entirely a
different nature, for these are of the different developments. As
we find, that would be illustrated in conditions of individuals
born in the material world, on the same moment. One in East,
one in West. The different environment under which the persona
would manifest would partake of the environment, yet there
would be similar conditions in the earth plane to each entity."
(900–22)

"[Entities] that enter an experience as a complete cycle; that is, upon the same period under the same astrological experiences as in the sojourn just before [that is, being born upon the same day of month—though time may have been altered]; find periods of activity that will be very much the same as those manifested in the previous sojourn, in the unfoldment and in the urges latent and manifested." (2814-1)

If at first you don't succeed, try, try and try again.

Do not, however, allow your astrological chart to *rule* your life, no matter how precisely it was drawn up for "from astrological aspects [so-called] it might be said that it gets about all the good there is in it. For various individuals, under various cycles of course, are subject to various changes as they pass through the various periods of the zodiac. But most astrological reflexes are about three to four degrees or periods off with many individuals. . . .

"This is not belittling astrological influences, just showing the inconsistency at times." (3688-1) "If a composite were made of the urges arising from the sojourns during the interims between material (earth) experiences, or the astrological aspects, we find certain inclinations. For these, the astrological aspects, represent the interims between the material or earth awarenesses. For the soul, to be sure, is aware and active in other consciousnesses than the three dimensional. For as the soul is in this particular solar system, it is subject to and active in all those phases of awareness in same. Some call it astrology, some call it foolishness; yet as indicated, these influences do not supplant the will." (3062-2)

The question which arises in many minds is why—why go through all these experiences? "For without passing through each and every stage of development, there is not the correct vibration to become one with the Father. . . . Then in the many stages of development throughout the universe or in the great system of the Universal Forces, each stage of development is made manifest through flesh—which is the testing portion of the Universal Vibration. In this manner, then, and for this reason, all are made manifest in flesh and there is the development through aeons of time and space, called eternity." (900–16)

Speaking of the man known as Jesus, and describing the route taken until the Christing in the earth plane, Cayce gave: "When the soul reached that development in which it reached earth's plane, it became in the flesh the model, as it had reached through the developments in those spheres, or planets, known in the earth's plane, obtaining the One in All.

> As in Mercury pertaining of Mind.
> As in Mars of Madness.
> In Earth as of Flesh.
> In Venus as Love.
> In Jupiter as Strength.
> In Saturn as the beginning of Earthly Woes, that to which all insufficient matter is cast for the beginning. [The weaver of patterns of response].
> In that of Uranus as of the Psychic.
> In that of Neptune as of Mystic.
> In Septimus as of Consciousness.
> In Arcturus as of the Developing."

(900–10)

Moving from one state of being—or consciousness—to another, back to God.

The influences of the planets according to Cayce agreed and disagreed with the accepted interpretations—but then our astrologers agree and disagree with one another today. For those who are astrologically inclined, a deeper and more complete study of the references made in the readings would be a rewarding project. "That the astrological sojourns are a portion of an entity's experience is exemplified oft by the sages, in their study and understanding of the elemental forces; yet such urges do not ever surpass the will's influence in the experience of an entity. That what is constructive in its spiritual import must and does become a portion of the individuality, and is a sign through the personality of an entity—and may be used, *never* abused. For such are the signs along the way, and indicate to an entity the road that has been taken." (824–1)

Q. "How can I use the astronomical, the numerical, the environs of the creations in the vibrations from metal, from stones, which influence me, to advantage in my present life?"

A. "As these are but lights, but signs in thine experience, they are as but a candle that one stumbles not in the dark. But worship NOT the light of the candle; rather that to which it may guide thee in thy service. So, whether from the vibrations from numbers, of metals, of stones, these are merely to become the necessary influence to make thee in attune, one with the Creative Forces; just as the pitch of a song of praise is not the song nor the message therein, but is a helpmeet for those that would find strength in the service of the Lord. So use them to attune self. How, ye ask? AS YE APPLY, YE ARE GIVEN THE NEXT STEP." (707–2)

Realizing the full scope of outside influences can be rather staggering. When we think of the world reduced to its atomic level, and realize that every atom is vibrating in its own frequency to hold itself in relation to its fellow atoms and create the form which we see and know, some sense can be made of all this. The Hindus call the world—or earth—*maya*, illusion. Atoms vibrating at such and such a frequency create the illusion of a tree, and others the illusion of a bird. All in reality is simply *energy*, the lowest common denominator of everything that is, the movement of the first cause. Matter is merely "an expression of Spirit in motion." (262–78)

Do we have any safety factors built into our being? Case 2670 was told: "In the way and manner—will the *love* counsel be rather the ruling factor, these will protect; for *every* individual has what may be *termed* [from the material plane] its own guardian angel, or influence. *Love* and *its* effects guards *this* entity. Depend upon the force in love's influence."

From this we see that our guardian angel does not have to be in the form of a personality or discarnate being. In her case it was in the form of an attitude. Love. How many other safety factors might there be of which we are not aware?

Fear not for influences, for know that "no urge is greater than the influence of mind over circumstance." (5377-1)

Study your strengths and weaknesses from the stars. Wear your favorite gem, your favorite perfume, and have a fresh flower pinned over your heart. Walk in an aura of your most harmonious colors while humming a happy tune, and cause all around you to smile and be happy. It is up to you to make the world a brighter place, so USE YOUR INFLUENCE!

*And it shall come to pass afterward, that I
will pour out my spirit upon all flesh; and
your sons and your daughters shall prophesy,
your old men shall dream dreams, your young
men shall see visions . . .* JOEL 2:28

WORKING YOUR WAY THROUGH NIGHT SCHOOL

SIGMUND FREUD stunned the minds of his contemporaries to a
new state of wakefulness when he expounded upon the importance of dreams and their interpretation in seeking to know ourselves. His message came into an era that was turning toward
the scientific exploration of the mind and away from the mystic.

But now that Freud has become a household word, the trend
seems to be turning back to the mystic and we can see in many
excerpts from the Bible the role that dream interpretation
played in the days of the Hebrew prophets.

First mentioned was Joseph, whose gift of interpretative insight took him out of the dungeon where he had seen in the
dreams of the pharaoh's butler and baker the prophecy of a
great famine. This power to read the meaning of dreams gave
him importance in the pharaoh's court and saved his people.

"It was in a dream that the Lord appeared to Solomon and
granted him an understanding heart." (I Kings, 3:5)

The dreams that troubled Nebuchadnezzar were beginning to
trouble his whole kingdom. His magicians, astrologers and sor-

cerers had failed to satisfy him with adequate interpretations and he was about to destroy all the wise men of Babylon. Realizing that the wisdom to reveal the meaning of so important a dream would not come from the cleverness of a wise man's mind, Daniel sought divine guidance and received it in a 'night vision' saying to the king: "But there is a God in heaven that revealeth secrets and maketh known . . . what shall be in the latter days." (Daniel 2:28)

In dreams we communicate with an intelligence infinitely higher than our own conscious state. It has been delicately intimated throughout this book—and told more bluntly in the Cayce readings—that if we didn't put up such well-insulated barriers between ourselves and the creative forces, all things we asked could be ours. This power can only come when we have arrived at a state of consciousness in which we will be able to handle it. It is only by the grace of God that it is withheld, for if received in a state of selfish desires, it would be to our further undoing.

Man's free will—God's gift—the positive charge (atomically speaking), when active will repel man from God automatically. Man seeks assistance and guidance, but can seldom put aside his will long enough to receive it. When asked what the Bible's most important message was, Cayce replied, "It is not God's will that any soul should perish." Bearing this in mind, it is feasible that guidance could be sought at any opportune moment. It is in meditation that man relinquishes his will, as well as in sleep.

Many dreams are prophetic, others just hint at better attitudes which might be adopted. Some dreams act merely as encouragements while others advise definite actions for the individual if he is to remain healthy.

It is not the purpose of this chapter to delve into the physiology of dreams—for with the research that is being done today, anything said in a scientific vein might be obsolete tomorrow. Suffice it to say that a dream laboratory has been set up at Maimonides Hospital in New York, where extensive tests are being made.

For the basic understanding of dreams some guideposts will be given here, but the more serious student will wish to explore the subject in the writings of Freud, Jung, Cayce and Elsie Sechrist.

In order to understand what dreams are, it would be well to get a clear picture of what sleep is. "Sleep is that period of time when the soul takes stock of what it has acted upon from one rest period to another; drawing comparisons—as it were—which comprise life itself in its essence." (5754-2)

Cayce tried to impress many times that all food which is ingested is not necessarily assimilated, as all experiences are not digested into the electrical patterns which constitute a body. And many times undigested food may even be the cause of certain dreams. "There are dreams which are produced by conditions of the digestive system of the physical body—to which little credence may be given, except as to the physical condition of the entity gaining such impressions, for these are in reality dreams." (900-13)

From this we understand that the dream may give the dreamer special knowledge into what is happening in his physical body. Many instances of physical advice have been reported at ARE study groups, where dream interpretation is an integral part of the program. Advice may be given as to diet, rest habits (or lack of them), certain vitamins or minerals which are lacking in the system, and, most important of all, attitudes to be adopted having a direct bearing on the health.

In sleep certain bodily functions are slowed down to a degree. The senses are suspended—although Cayce suggested that the sense of hearing remained alert, and the sixth sense was alerted.

What is the sixth sense? "The forces or activity of the soul itself . . . for the soul is the body, or the spiritual essence of an entity manifested in this material plane." (5754-2)

Sleep is an extremely important part of the health of an individual. If its true worth were known there would be fewer people patronizing nightclubs, and the late night talk shows would enjoy a far lower rating. The secret here is that "the whole organism of the human body is made up of such electronic forces as is necessary for sufficient in that called sleep to recuperate the energies of the whole body." (1800–4)

Shakespeare made the poetic observation that sleep knitted up the ravelled sleeve of care. If those dedicated individuals who insist on continuing their workaday activities through bouts of flu and cold would stay home in bed and allow the body to gather its forces for healing, they would not have to wonder why colds and flu hang on. (They might also help their fellow man to enjoy less exposure to infection.) We are told that with one tiny pill, which covers the symptoms of a cold, we are fit enough to continue living in the same old way. Who is kidding whom? If the body were allowed to rest—and that does not mean to overfeed it; the organs need to rest too—it has the power to balance itself. This does not suggest that all ailments can be treated by going to bed, but a multitude of minor ailments with which we are plagued might be more easily alleviated should one take to the bed for a period.

An old friend from Atlanta reminisced that in the deep South, it was a practice for the lady of the estate to spend one day a week in bed. It was known as 'Missy's Day In Bed' and Missy literally spent the whole day in bed, sick or not. She ate all her meals there, and if guests appeared they would visit her in the bedroom. Why have our lives become so frantic? Even the Lord rested on the seventh day; might we not schedule an early night at least once a week?

In sleep, not only does our body rest and get the important resuscitation it needs, but our conscious mind turns itself off as well. "When the physical body lies in slumber, we find the organs that are subjugated, the life-giving flow and the subconscious forces acting, and the soul forces ready for that communication with intermingling conditions lying between." (900–10)

To interpret a dream, we have to remember it. You may say that you never dream, but science tells us that we all dream for at least two hours each night. This is supported by evidence of tests made in the dream laboratory using electroencephalograms, or EEGs. The rapid eye movements, or REMs, as they are called, signify a subconscious activity (dreaming) and their regularity is carefully noted. If when going to sleep one knows that it is imperative to awaken at a certain time, one usually does—maybe seconds before the alarm goes off. If when going to sleep one impresses the mind with the fact that the dream must be remembered, the memory of it will be brought back to consciousness. Often, the most salient parts of the dream carry the essence of the message.

One piece of important advice to the would-be student of dreams: have a pad and a pencil on the bedside table and write the dream down the moment you awaken. Should you wake during the night with a dream and postpone writing it down till the morning, it is as good as lost. Write it down immediately, and remember as many details as you can: positioning of things in the dream, colors, shapes, and the most important of all—your feelings about the dream.

Dreams can be so straightforward as to leave no doubt about their meaning, while at other times they may appear obtuse, as fraught with symbolism as an Egyptian tomb. Why?

A symbol is a composite of understanding coming from the subconscious whose meaning often cannot be limited to words. A message given in symbols necessitates a thorough look into the complicated corridors of our unconscious, and in the analysis comes our absorption of their meaning. "Dreams are of many natures. Dreams as we have given, are either from the material activity of individual influences attempting to be assimilated, or warring with those influences within the body, and bring visions or experiences that are at times called nightmares, night horses or the like. Those are experiences, also through which the subconscious forces are constantly aware of what has been the experience, and it comes as an influence for foreseeing or for premonition of experiences. And necessarily, unless they are impressed more than once become rather as dreams.

"Then there are experiences of the soul that has been awakened to the knowledge which has or may be written upon same, the experiences of an entity as an entity through its sojourns

. . . and these are given then in emblems or in visions that are to be and are a part of the individual entity." (281-27)

This gives us an understanding of why we may be in the garb of an Italian fisherman in our dream, or maybe in a situation which seemed so 'at home' and yet, upon awakening, seems a lifetime away. Messages come to us through our dreams from past experiences in which we set up situations to be worked out in this experience.

There are some guides to the understanding of dreams which came through the Cayce readings that parallel the findings of others involved in the study of dreams. It is most important to remember that in interpreting dreams, you are the dreamer. The feeling which you bring back from a dream is more important than anything which a dictionary of symbols has to say about what has happened in your dream. You are the ultimate judge. If you awake with a feeling of foreboding—be warned. If it is one of elation—carry it through your daily activities; it must be an important part of the message of the dream.

Sometimes the characters in your dream are themselves, but more often they are a facet of you; even those of the opposite sex become the opposing principle in yourself. Should there be another character in your dream whom you may know, ask yourself what this person represents to you.

There are certain symbols which are universally accepted—and to which interpretation you may eventually resort—but your feeling is of prime importance. When starting to study your dreams, it would be a good idea to study a dictionary of symbols.* For when studying any new language, it is a good idea, after having studied the rudimentary grammar, to build up as large a vocabulary as possible. It seems that when the subconscious realizes that you are serious in your desire to learn, having more symbols at your command, it will use them and your studies will be more fruitful.

Many people fear death in dreams. It is a wonderful symbol,

* Author's note: Both the Cirlot (parallels Gaskell's *Dictionary of Sacred Language of All Scriptures and Myths*) and Gaskell dictionaries are excellent.

to be welcomed rather than feared, representing the death of a cycle through which one has passed, the opening of a new door. It can be the death of a bad habit, a false ideal, or of a karmic tie to a situation which has been hounding us in the form of a memory pattern, for literally ages.

A birth is something to rejoice in, as it is in the conscious life. One dreams of carrying a babe, a developing life pattern, a new ideal. Sometimes the birth will take place signifying that a new situation, ideal or set of values has materialized. If the child is beautiful, nurture it (the ideal), if it is monstrous, take heed and question yourself.

Water is a frequent part of our dreams, and why not? It is our source, as it is the source of all life. Is the water clean or muddy? How do we react to the water; do we fear it or are we a part of it? Are we afloat on the water in a boat just large enough for one, or is it an ocean-going liner?

If water is the source of all life, the fish is its indwelling spirit. Early Christians used the sign of the fish to identify themselves, to one another. The zodiacal sign of the Christ (Pisces) is that of two fishes, reversed. Twin principles—opposites—negative and positive.

When a symbol appears in your dream, before running to the dictionary of symbols, first dissect it in *your* mind. If, for example, a palm tree appears as one of the important symbols in your dream, think of all the attributes of a palm tree. It gives shelter, it gives food: dates and coconuts. In a desert, it is the sign of the presence of water, an oasis.

What might mist mean to you? First of all, take it apart; it is air and water. Its outlines are nebulous, not clearly defined. The word itself connotes something partially hidden, maybe mysterious? Strange that makers of movies which deal with the occult or mysterious happenings usually open with a scene of mists rising about a swamp or castle in dreamlike surrealism.

Though your dreams may not always contain momentous prophecies, they can be a gold mine of little nuggets of precognition. Why not use dreams as an aid in overcoming problems before they arise; an ounce of prevention is worth a pound of cure. This ounce of prevention might be in the form of something to be added to your diet, or an attitude which will have an enormous effect upon a situation on the horizon. That vital key to understanding which has seemed hidden in the mists of time itself can be brought to light through our mastery of symbols. "Astrologically, we find latent and manifested urges arise from the vision, day dreams or dreams of the entity. These are manners and means through which those awarenesses are kept of man's soul being one with the Creative Forces.

"In these we find the indication of what the entity as an individual has done about its opportunities, its privileges; as there are the influences accredited to the various spheres or consciousnesses to and through which an entity passes in the interims between the sojourns of material consciousness. Then, they are awarenesses, and have their part in the character—yea, even the personality—yea even more the individuality of an entity." (2345-1)

As the more advanced books on symbology are stocked with references to such things as The Head of Horus on a Pole (symbol of aspiration), Ocypete, the Harpy (symbol of the love of physical life) and Cow's Milk Poured Out Toward the North (symbolic of wisdom), it would be remiss to allow ourselves to get caught up in dreamworld flamboyance and overlook the basic bread and butter symbols that are in most of our dreams.

Who has not dreamed about a car? This could represent the entity's body, the vehicle of the soul in the earth plane. Ask yourself: Was the car a functional one, or large and splashy? Was the road traveled smooth or rocky, narrow or wide? Was it a high road or a low road? WERE YOU DRIVING THE CAR or was somebody else driving it; if so, who? Were you searching for a parking place; did you find one? Were you able to apply the brakes at the right moment?

Another all-star regular is a house, which on one level could represent a state of consciousness. Is the house a mansion or a hovel? Maybe it is a hotel where transients stay. Does the house belong to you? Is it your ideal house or just a make-do until the right thing comes along? What shape of house is it? Is it on a mountaintop or in a valley? What color is it? Does the action take place upstairs or downstairs (often the attic is the higher mental faculties and the basement might be the *sub*-conscious where things may be hidden away).

Animals can refer to our animal nature. If a dog appears as a lovable fluffy puppy, it might mean that we are not yet ready to relinquish our instincts. Think of the traits of other animals which frequent your dreams and how they might apply to your life. Animals often represent an archetype of a state of consciousness, *i.e.* the fox is cunning, the lion majestic and the eel slippery.

Birds are spirits incarnate. They represent the flight of the aspirations of the individual. Their specific traits depend upon the type of bird as well as what it was doing in the dream and what we might think about birds. Birds can be messengers (carrier pigeons) or predators.

Hair can mean thoughts. Does your dream deal with the cutting of hair (cutting off certain thoughts) or the curling or dressing of thoughts? Is the hair in the front of the head or the back? What color is the hair? All may be significant.

The mouth is a source of trouble for so many of us. A big mouth means just that. Teeth can bite, biting words—as false teeth can mean false words. The tongue, although an organ of taste, has been spoken of as having the power to sting (tongue lashing). Free associate with its various functions.

Fear of heights is often experienced in dreams. One explanation can be that one is ascending to a realm above the present state and fears the responsibility. The higher we attain, the farther we have to fall. It may be a test of our faith.

Going to the bathroom in one's dream can mean an urgent need coming through from the conscious state, or the symbol of inner cleansing. This is a frequent symbol and one to be greeted as an old friend.

Any form of policeman is the representation of the higher law, the universal law. It is a law which can never be escaped or hoodwinked as so many of our earthly laws can be. We are forever watched by our higher selves, which may be represented as a judge in our dreams.

Theaters and movie houses can show us our immediate environment, the stage of life—for are we not all merely players? However, the scenes portrayed are more than entertainment. Watch them closely. Note: Who is the director? The star? The audience?

Sex in dreams can refer to just that, but not always. Very often the sexual act or marriage (wedding) can mean the union of one part of the self with another. The integration of the many aspects of ourselves is important to a full and healthy life. Often one's subdued sexual preferences or longings emerge in the dream state, but, remembering that we have had many lives in many guises which are built into our being, we must not be too severe in our judgment. Rather we should spiritualize what we have now and line upon line build a healthier view.

Flying is a favorite dream of many people. It can represent soaring above the day's cares and woe, an escape from it all. It can mean that we are receiving the suggestion to view our problems from a height from which we see them in their proper perspective, instead of being immersed in them. Or it may be that we are taking a quick flight around in our astral bodies (astral projecting).

The bed can stand for at least three things: healing, sex and rest, and more if you can think of them. If the bed is in a hospital, there is no question. A hospital is a place of healing, a state of consciousness which heals. Or the bed could represent rest, that most important ingredient to good health which leads to beauty.

Have you ever dreamed of trying to get 'home'? You search for a bus or a taxi and sometimes find yourself at an airport trying to get reservations on a plane. Perhaps you are yearning for your spiritual home.

When analyzing your dreams, write them down, remembering as many details as possible. It may sound silly to you at the time of writing it, but when you return to it, maybe with your morning cup of herb tea, write down 'your' meaning of as many of the symbols which you can pick out, and then go through it again. Very often the revelations which come make one laugh with the sheer wonder of knowing that guidance can come from one's dreams.

One need not be a Jungian analyst to start seeking help from dreams. All you need is a pencil and paper and some determination to try. It is a fascinating study and one which grows with use (as will your facility in interpretation). Date your dreams and you will be able to check back later and see how many of them were prophetic. You may discover yourself to be one of the prophets of the Aquarian Age.

The magna cum laude of dreaming is awarded to one who can interpret his dream while still in the dream state. The Oriental sage Chen Chi Chang is noted to have said: "He who remains in control of his dreams in dreaming, is in control of his states of being in the afterlife."

This may sound too funny to be true but a dear friend of mine traveled to India to visit the exiled Dalai Lama of Tibet to receive this identical information.

Maeterlinck displayed great wisdom in his tale of the Bluebird of Happiness: one can travel the world in search of it only to find it in his own backyard.

CHAPTER *14* *Rejuvenation*

CAYCE READINGS AND MODERN RESEARCH

WHAT PRICE are you willing to pay to recapture your youth? Before you laugh at the idea of Faust selling his soul to the devil for the elixir of youth, think of the lengths to which modern man has resorted to find just such an antidote to aging.

Those who are not only willing but able to *pay* for the ultimate in beauty services might spend a full day each week enduring inumerable discomforts in the name of youth and beauty. A top-to-toe session at one of our luxury beauty salons would surely appear to Faust as a scene from a medieval torture chamber. Within these gilded walls what techniques are available to camouflage, preserve, dye, peel, stretch and bend the fortunate recipient toward her desired goal?

First of all, the client could be given a facial which might include a peeling of the outer layer of her skin by massaging it with a lotion containing powdered pumice, a practice which started in ancient Greece. The purpose here is to remove dead cells on the skin's surface and speed the cycle of cell renewal.

Next, under the guise of strengthening the body and facial muscles, she subjects herself to mild electrical shocks. Should the hair be graying, it would be dyed—often by first stripping the natural color from the hair and reintroducing the preferred color to the hair shaft. After the normal tortures of perming, rolling and drying, if her night out is to be a special one, she might resort to the 'skyhooks.' These are clamping devices, cunningly concealed behind the hairline to stretch the loose skin tightly over the bones. For a lesser occasion, a temporary wrinkle-smoother made from bovine albumen can be applied underneath the make-up. This is a solidifying gelatinous substance which, applied to the face, feels something like glue.

Should these measures still leave something to be desired, the next step is plastic surgery.

Plastic surgery has become more and more popular in this age of affluence and youth-worship. There are now available complete surgical face-lifts, mini-lifts, eye surgery (often performed in the surgeon's office) for drooping lids and pouches under the eyes. Rhinoplasty—changing the shape of the nose surgically—is an accepted practice; often the chin is built up at the same time to maintain the balance of feature. No part of the human body has been left unexplored by the plastic surgeon.

For an entertainer or someone who is constantly in the public's eye, this can be understood. For the average man or woman —if there are any average people left in the world—a question is posed: Why?

One would not seek to change oneself if one were at peace. If happiness were the order of the day—every day—who would want to change? The question we must now ask ourselves is: 'Will this altered appearance bring us happiness'? Will it solve any of the problems which beset us? Will it bring us the peace and security that we desire?

If rejuvenation is what you are after, look no further, for Edgar Cayce said that "THERE NEED NOT BE EVER THE NECESSITY OF A PHYSICAL ORGANISM AGING." (1299-1)

How did Cayce's suggestions for rejuvenation go along with some of today's practices? While reading his words it is difficult to believe that he died over twenty-five years ago; his wisdom is timeless.

Case 2533-6 sought an outline for living which would insure

longevity. "In giving a discourse upon how this entity may extend the life expectancy, with a mind-body activity in keeping with the conditions to which the entity may hope to attain—to be sure each entity, each soul, is in many respects a law unto itself; especially as related to the activities and the diets that would extend or impel life expectancy."

As diet has already been dealt with, consider these few dietary aids to longevity: "A form of vitamin may be obtained from certain nuts—as the almond—that would be helpful as a preventative. Also there may be obtained from the turtle egg those influences for longevity that may be created in certain cellular forces in the body." (659-1)

Vitamin E, which is sometimes known as the virility vitamin, has met with great success in the health food markets of the world. Cayce advised for breakfast: "fresh fruits that are used with the various cereals carrying an extraordinary amount of vitamins—as Vitamin E, Vitamin D, Vitamin E especially, will react wtih the *regenerative* forces of the system." (4246-1)

Maintaining virility—whether through therapeutic doses of vitamins or hormone shots, blood radiation or whatever—is the goal of all men seeking a prolonged youth. Nothing, however, has created quite the sensation of Voronoff and his monkey glands.

In the earlier half of this century, Serge Voronoff gained great favor among the older wealthy set by transplanting the testes of monkeys to increase the sexual activity in the male—which in turn would rejuvenate the woman in his life.

An attempt was made to transplant the monkeys from Africa to the Voronoff 'singerie' at the base of his palatial chateau on the Italian Riviera, but later it was found that the recipients of the glands were also the recipients of syphilis, with which the monkeys were infected. Serge Voronoff went into hiding with his crumpled dream and died shortly after.

Perhaps the most celebrated and longest-lived treatments have been cellular therapy. In a nutshell: through blood and other tests, it is determined which organs or glands are functioning below their maximum efficiency; these organs are then dissected from freshly killed sheep's fetuses, finely chopped and put into a saline solution for injection into the ailing patient. This presumably goes straight to the failing organ and regenerates it. Cells are also available in a dried form, but the fresh are the preferred. These treatments have been enjoyed by many wealthy celebrities. What might Cayce have thought of this treatment?

Cayce agreed that "the healing must come from within—that is, life force—or cell units—must build within, or from within, in such a way and manner as to bring resuscitating life energy through the whole system." (5440–1)

But he did not totally approve of the methods, for "this regeneration may not come about by merely injections or extracts or compounds to react, but must come as a gradual growth of the expression and coordination of the nervous systems and the physical reactions to creative and regenerative forces within the body-functionings themselves." (2248–1) "For, the ability of each functioning of the body forces is to reproduce itself, and as long as this continues, the body keeps not only young but active—mentally, spiritually, physically—unless it be drugged by its own ego." (3042–1)

A woman need not think that because her reproductive faculties have ceased her cells cease their regeneration.

Q. "If women followed correct diet and lived properly, could menopause be postponed till seventy or entirely eliminated?"

A. "This is a natural source as from the Divine Forces, and is the natural consequence of those conditions from the First Cause—though by the continued effort there might be such a thing accomplished in the tenth generation. But for what purpose, if God ordained otherwise?" (1158–33)

Cayce insisted that our cells are constantly changing, and that every seven years each cell in our body is renewed. Working on this assumption Cayce suggested treatments for ailments which are still baffling the medical profession. It was necessary however to bring one's whole life into alignment. As far as our physical, mental and spiritual bodies are concerned, there could be no robbing Peter to pay Paul, for we are both Peter and Paul.

Rejuvenation, Cayce style, could be likened to a seven year plan. But do not become disheartened, the results start appearing almost immediately in one way or another. "All portions of the body come under varied cycles as changes are wrought. For the body fully and completely changes in seven years. Yet this is something continually going on, and various portions change at various reflex periods." (3688-1)

We must believe this, see it happening within us as this consciously directs our energy and speeds the process. "Remember, the body does gradually renew itself constantly. Do not look upon the conditions which have existed as not being able to be eradicated in the system. . . . Hold to that *knowledge*—and don't think of it as just theory—that the body CAN, the body DOES renew itself!

"Then keep those portions of the body active that do this; and we will find these conditions will—in a little while—be a thing of the past." (1548-3)

Here is more food for thought and contemplation; it was given for 3684-1: "For the body renews itself, every atom, in seven years. How have ye lived for the last seven? And then the seven before? What would ye do with thy mind and thy body if they were wholly restored to normalcy in this experience? Would these be put to the use of gratifying thine own appetites as at first? Will these be used for the magnifying of the appreciation of the love to the Infinite? For who healeth all thy diseases?"

Q. "Is it possible for our bodies to be rejuvenated in this incarnation?"

A. "Possible. For, as the body is an atomic structure, the units of energy around which there are movements of the atomic forces that—as given—are ever the sentiment or pattern of a Universe, as these atoms, as these structural forces are made to conform or to rely upon or to be one with the spiritual import, the spiritual activity, they revivify, they make for constructive forces." (262-85)

Q. Why is old age so dreaded and feared? What does one expect with old age? Case 5226-1 asked how she could overcome the fear of advancing years and being alone. She was told:

A. "By going out and doing something for others, that is, those who are not able to do for themselves; making others happy, forgetting self entirely. These fears are material manifestations and in helping someone else you'll get rid of them."

Q. "How can *I* help?"

A. "As to thy service—as to thy light unto others: Who may tell a rose how to be beautiful? Who may tell the stars or the moon in their courses how to raise within man's heart and soul the longing to know the Creator of ALL?" (2600-1) "For the greatest help for this body, let it use the abilities to bring better conditions for someone else. For each soul should learn to help itself and someone else. To have love, give it. To have friends, give friendship. To be healed, rid self of conditions which have produced difficulties." (5042-1)

Q. "How can I best prepare for old age?"

A. "By preparing for the present. Let old age only ripen thee. For one is ever just as young as the heart and the purpose. Keep sweet. Keep friendly. Keep loving, if ye would keep young." (3420-1)

Q. "Will my life in this plane be very long?"

A. "As long as it is used in constructive forces, it may be as long as desired." (2326-1)

Q. "How long will I be able to continue in work I am doing?"

A. "Just how long do you wish to continue? There will be others who will have to care for it when you are not here. Don't let this disturb you, because you will live as long as you desire to do good for others." (5223-1)

The last three questions and answers should leave no doubt in the mind as to Cayce's philosophy about aging. The more we do for others, the less conscious we are of ourselves. The friendlier and more loving we are, the less will others be aware of our advancing age. And as for longevity, we may live as long as we desire if we have something constructive toward which we may channel our energy. Our bodies may remain as young and vital as our needs to fulfill our purposes. "[A body] may remain in the physical as long as the ability lies within self to so apply the forces from without and within as to build or bring resuscitation to all forces from within, and, as desire is the father of *activity*, so is that brought *into* activity become life itself. Nothing grows, nothing remains alone unless dead. A mind, a body that sits alone and considers the outside and never turning that within to the out, nor that without from within, soon finds *drosses* setting up in the system; for development is change. Change is the activity of knowledge from within, Learn to *live!* Then there is no death, save the transition, when desired, see?" (900-465)

When we feel drained—as though our batteries were completely discharged—here is a routine, given to 1554-4, which sounds custom-made. "Relax the body fully just before attempting same, by repose. Then a little head and neck exercise. And after such experiences AGAIN a thorough relaxing, with plenty of water taken internally, and a little head and neck exercise; and we will find the responses to quick recuperative forces.

"In the activities of the physical forces of the body, those mental energies expended in carrying impressions as from individual to individual in the form of words or an activity sufficient for the comprehending in the minds of others, one often draws upon one's nervous energy: which becomes, to be sure, by posture, localized in the upper cervical or through the neck, between the shoulders—the head.

"Yet with the general exercises—that is—the circular motion of the head; backward; forward; to the sides—and with water, these produce, as it were, a recharging of the battery forces of the bodily functionings."

The exercise extolled as the "best exercise" is walking, "and in the *open* as much as possible. Not too great an amount of course, but sufficient activities to prevent the settling of any of the drosses or used energies that are not eliminated from settling in any portion of the system." (4633-1)

Q. Why in the open as much as possible?

A. "The entity should keep close to all of those things that have to do with outdoor activities, for it is the best way to keep yourself young—to stay close to nature, close to those activities in every form of exercise that breathe into thine own soul, as you would a sunset or a morning sun rising. And see that sometimes—it's as pretty as the sunset!" (3374-1)

We can apply the forces of nature in the rejuvenation of our minds and bodies once we understand the basic principles. "Know then that force in nature that is called electrical or electricity is that same force ye worship as creative or God in action!" (1299-1)

Cayce psychically designed and recommended a certain appliance. Despite its appearance—one of an electrical nature—"the vibrations from the appliance only use the energies of the body." (5326-1) For "as we find, all energy is electrical in its activity in a manifested form." (735-1)

But "this appliance is not electrical save by the changing of the vibratory forces from the bodily sources themselves." (1480-1) "In the . . . appliance the *body* builds the charge to be discharged through the instrument into other portions of the body." (1800-28) "[Its purpose] is to create *vibrations* as is set up

in blood and nerve system—for all life is of a vibratory nature—
the coordinating of vibrations sets a body in order." (4309–1)

A positive wire is attached to a pulse point at one extremity
of the body and to the appliance at the other. A negative wire
is attached to the pulse point at the opposite extreme on the
body and to the appliance.* The body's energies (vibrations)
are fed into the machine—where the vibrations are impeded or
slowed down—and then back into the body through the negative pole. After a short while, the vibrations of the body are
equalized. The coordination then of the superficial and deep
circulation brings for "more uniform heating forces—as it were
—in the system." (5557–1)

Q. "How to revitalize my nervous system?"

A. "Use that re-ionizer, the . . . appliance as has been given.
This *revitalizes* the system throughout! For it coordinates impulses." (1472–2)

Another way to use the appliance is to break the negative connection and feed it through a 'solution jar'. This jar may
contain any one of a number of solutions depending upon the
needs of the body. The solution itself was not introduced to
the body in other than vibrational form. It is up to the body
to manufacture its own chemicals or activities from the vibrations introduced. There were a variety of solutions suggested
for a variety of complaints. But our immediate concern is rejuvenation and the solutions recommended for this were gold
chloride and silver nitrate. Gold chloride solution was claimed
to aid any condition that bordered on rheumatics "or of the
necessity of rejuvenating any organ of the system showing the
delinquency in action, see?" (1800–6) The silver nitrate solution
is a nerve stimulant.

Cayce told 120–5 that "given properly, silver and gold may al-

_____

* Author's note: Positive and negative are relative terms here, since the
appliance is not a source of electricity.

most lengthen life to its double." A great deal of research will be necessary to determine what constitutes the "proper" application of the gold and silver—but where there is a silver lining, there is hope. "How few there be that a few dollars would not heal many, many a feeling . . . at least bring security! Then may not that spiritual force, with the knowledge of the *essences* of same as applied to the physical body, be applied in a *spiritual* manner as to bring efficacy in its *spiritual* application? The same as in Gold, that is a renewal; while Silver is a sustaining cord, a renewer of the energies as applied between the physical forces and the energies of activity in life itself upon nerve and brain forces as well as the very essence of the glandular secretions of the body." (281-27)

Within the last few years, medicine has discovered that gold has still untapped powers for healing. Experiments were made in hospitals—among them the Georgetown University Hospital in Washington, D.C.—with the use of gold leaf for dressing skin ulcers, bedsores and severe burns. The results were miraculous on open wounds which had previously resisted all other treatments.*

The following speaks for itself: "Many ills are results of alcoholic stimulants. These have destroyed tissue in the central portions of the body; destroyed tissues in the generative system, in other places and in the brain itself. Gold and silver are good for this, for they rejuvenate the system." (1800-6)

The relaxation experienced by researchers of this appliance has been unparalleled. This is an appliance "for bringing rest to the weary, rest to those who have been inclined to depend upon sedatives and narcotics to rest; to those who have been under great periods of stress and strain; to those who seek to find an equalizing influence that will assist them in producing a coordination in their physical and mental beings with the spiritual affluence and effect of its activity of spirituality upon the body physical." (1800-28)

* Reported in the *Journal of the American Medical Association;* Vol. 196— page 693.

Case 1663-1 was told: "But even when these [disturbances] disappear, do not leave off those periods of rest, when there is the raising of the creative energies and forces within the body—through the use of the . . . appliance, which, as indicated, is to equalize impulse by the very use of energies within the own body."

The appliance was also used in conjunction with other treatments to increase the body's receptivity to these treatments upon all levels. Case 1016-1 had tissues which had broken down on the left side of her face and wanted to know what could be done to build them up. She was told: "A massage with the electrically driven vibrator, followed immediately with a compound massaged through the neck, the side of the face, through the eyes, the temple, and along the vagus centers (right at the entrance of the gullet, or at the entrance of the shoulder blade, or corner of the shoulder blade with the breast bone on either side). Such a compound for massaging would be prepared in this manner:

"To one tablespoonful of melted Cocoa Butter, add—while it is in the liquid:

> 1 tbsp. Rose Water
> 1 tbsp. Compound Tincture of Benzoin

Keep this to massage into these tissues. The activity of these ingredients will be to enliven and to make for—well, this would be a very very good skin cleanser and skin builder for *anyone!*

"Do these. At the period of taking the [recommended] appliance we would keep the constructive attitude . . . or meditate, building toward the coordination of the vibratory forces from the energies of the cosmic forces to the active forces of a mental and spiritual body. This will *aid* materially when such applications are taken.

"For the vibrations created by the use of the appliance are the natural forces with the activities of the system being attuned to those from without, bringing to the body the better vibrations. Thus we create an equalized circulating, and . . . with the addition of the other properties in their proper ratio and form as indicated . . . bring *uniformity* to the activity of organs, glands and the eliminations of the body, which makes for normalcy in health." "And if the body were to use the [recommended] appliance in the lower forces to the extremities, it may keep its body in almost *perfect* accord for many-many-many-MANY days." (823-1)

This appliance is presently being researched in many areas and may hold the key to the solution of numerous problems which are tormenting mankind.

Q. "Does patting of the tissues of the face help to keep muscles from sagging or are the facial exercises better?

A. "It does. The patting of the tissues is the better." (811-4)

For those of you whose practice it is to stand before the mirror each morning or evening and make funny faces at yourselves— you can relax and start patting.

Case 1947-4 asked how sagging muscles can be avoided and how corrected. She was told: "By massage, and the use of those creams as indicated over the chin and throat, around the eyes, and such conditions. Occasionally the use of the Boncilla or mud packs would be very good."

"How can people avoid aging in appearance?" she then asked. "The mind" was the answer.

Which of the laws of the universe explained in the Cayce readings might apply to this last statement? The law of expectancy. "The expectancy of the physical body must be awakened before the body, through its tissue, its vital forces, can emanate the necessary building, or eliminating forces, of the physical body, to rebuild or develop properly." (900-21) "Know that even at this period in the experience of the body there is that within the body which *will* replenish, if the body is kept cleansed from the impurities of poor eliminations." (1464-1)

The law of expectancy could even govern our leaving this

world. Isn't it true that we expect to die at a certain age? Why? Methuselah lived nine hundred and sixty-nine years, and Moses didn't do too badly at one hundred and twenty, considering that when he died "his eye was not dim, nor his natural forces abated" (Deut. 34:7). Moses *could* not die until he had fulfilled what he had set out to do. He expected to see the promised land—although admittance was denied him—and he lived until it was possible.

As long as you have a goal, a motivating force to spur you on, there can be no stopping you, unless you build a short circuit into your mechanism with negativity. Cayce told us to be outdoors, spend time with nature, breathe it into our very soul. Might it have been advised with the hope that we would learn a lesson from nature? We have urges in our bodies, indeed in each and every cell. Cayce told us that each cell contained the universe. Difficult for some to imagine, but with inner searching may come the answer for "the well of truth, yea the fountain of eternal life, wells up from within." (1580-1)

Should we find these urges directed in the wrong way, "The *urges* are not beyond being changed. For as one views the activities about one in every nature, as in the laws of nature itself, one sees that it is a changing world. NOTHING stands still, it either advances through the laws that are applicable in its own state or stage of development, or is pushed aside by the general law of deterioration; that what is not in activity or expanding in energies—becomes changed for the entrance into those influences as ye call separation or death, or the rebirth of the growth; dependent upon the manner of its application or use." (1499-1)

Case 539-2 was "one capable of seeing beauty depicted in all expressions in nature, whether the bug about its lowly activity of cleansing the conditions about man, or the beauty of song in music, whether reed or string, or the beauty in the rose, the sunset, the stream, or in the awakening of nature as it illustrates to man the new birth into another experience in the material condition." "Thinkest thou that ANY of the influences of nature that you see about you—the acorn, the oak, the elm or the vine, or anything—has forgotten what manner of expression? Only man forgets." (294-189)

The acorn contains the oak. Could you imagine planting an acorn to grow a gladiola?

Of all the laws given to man to help guide his life through calmer waters, one, and only one, was called the 'golden rule.' "*As ye would that men should do to you, do ye so even for them.* It is simple in words, yet so deep in its meaning, so far reaching in its application in every phase of human experience!" (2170-1)

It is also the answer to that elusive quality captured by the great beauties of the world. "For according to the true law of spirit, like begets like. Thus as harmony and beauty and grace reign within the consciousness of an entity, it gives out such to others and others wonder what moves them to feel different, when no one spoke, no one appeared to be anxious. This is the manner in which the spirit of truth operates among the children of men." (3098-2)

To sum up then: The approach to beauty which may be drawn from the Edgar Cayce readings can start anywhere. The links in the chain of perfection may be explored in any order providing we do not lose sight of the fact that they do form a circle. This book deals firstly with the outer skin, the façade. One should recognize the importance of caring for the outer skin of both body and face. Care for the hair that it might truly be your crowning glory. Ascertain that your diet feeds every *part* of you and after assimilating all the food's benefits, make sure that you do not retain its waste matter. Do have regular periods of exercise and occasionally pamper yourself with a steam bath and massage. Realize that your mind can project health and beauty if you so program it. Recognize the strengths which can be drawn from the influences which surround us. Search your dreams for clues which may brighten your life and draw on every resource to remain young and vital.

No matter whose formula you follow, starting on a new beauty program and being faced with a hundred and one priceless gems of information can be a bit overwhelming if viewed as just another set of rules to further complicate your existence. Such a radical beauty program as Cayce outlined can be regarded as just another bothersome set of rules. On the other hand, it might be regarded by many as a sensible survival program through which they might surmount the distorted values that the marketplace has put on beauty.

Cayce's beauty program is nothing short of inspired. It is a way of life in itself, compatible with the natural existence which we are all innately seeking. Edgar Cayce, channeling the infinite wisdom, would not offer advice without also suggesting how it be applied, for until something is applied, it remains in the realm of the unmanifest.

The starting point need not remain nebulous. Remember that we must start right where we are, for the place upon which we are standing is holy. Do what you have at hand. Each of us, individual as we are, has something different at hand. Should your diet be at fault, concentrate on changing that first. Your first step could be simply to start the day with a glass of warm water or to eliminate the cream from your coffee. Perhaps your first step will be to start a daily period of exercise or to work toward better eliminations. A most essential part of any life which reflects a natural existence is the inner attunement which comes from a regular period of meditation each day. Even the glossy fashion magazines have reported on the beneficial effect of *actual* chemical changes in the body brought about by meditation—based on current research.

A beauty regime, as everything else, must be built line upon line; one's system should not be shocked by a complete, overnight turnabout. Thoughts which have taken many lifetimes to shape our mental bodies cannot be expected to disappear in a flash, but by changing habits slowly and purposefully, the mind can be reshaped as surely as can the body—with correct diet and exercise. The mind too may become a thing of beauty.

Never forget who you are—not the earthbound personality, for that is simply the vehicle of the eternal you during your present trip. Seek your true individuality which is waiting to be embraced, and allow it to guide you.

Now that you possess the component parts of beauty, the ingredients are yours to combine and enjoy. Life is the application of that known—so apply and reveal the beauty that is yours alone. Make the world a more beautiful place by your presence; it is your privilege, your gift from God—a gift you can return to Him through your fellow man.

Nearly all of the ingredients mentioned by Edgar Cayce are available without prescription from drug stores or supermarkets. The following is a list of some of the most frequently mentioned products:

ATOMIDINE. A water-soluble iodine compound. The manufacturer advertises it as active, non-toxic and non-irritating. Controlled to liberate one percent nascent iodine in solution. Contains one percent nascent iodine. Is not recommended for internal use except upon the advice of a physician.

BLACK AND WHITE COSMETICS. Brand name of a cosmetic line available in Cayce's time.

BONCILLA. Brand name for a cosmetic mud pack.

COCA-COLA. Soft drink usually mixed with carbonated water. The Cayce readings suggested to certain individuals that the syrup be mixed with non-carbonated water and taken at various intervals.

GLYCO-THYMOLINE. Treatment for mucosity, a mouthwash that has been on the market for many years. Distributed by Kress and Owens Company. Contains (according to label) sodium benzoate; sodium bicarbonate; borax; sodium salicylate; glycerine; eucalyptol; menthol; thymol; oil of sweet birch; oil of pine needles. Among manufacturer's suggested uses: Application for sunburn, insect bites, douche, throat and nasal spray. Cayce's recommendations for the internal use of this product never exceeded fifteen drops per day.

LISTERINE. Antiseptic. Alcohol content: twenty-five percent. Recommended for use by manufacturer as a gargle, mouthwash and for minor cuts and scratches, insect bites and infectious dandruff.

NUJOL.   An extra-heavy mineral oil.

WITCH HAZEL.   A mild astringent used for years as a skin lotion. It is an extract from the plant hamamelis.